Community School Mathematics 3A

Pat Lilburn
Pam Rawson
Peter Sullivan

Oxford University Press
Department of Education, Papua New Guinea

OXFORD
UNIVERSITY PRESS

Oxford University Press is a department of the University of Oxford. It furthers the University's objective of excellence in research, scholarship, and education by publishing worldwide. Oxford is a registered trademark of Oxford University Press in the UK and in certain other countries.

Published in Australia by
Oxford University Press
253 Normanby Road, South Melbourne, Victoria 3205, Australia

and

The Department of Education, Papua New Guinea

First published 1993
Reprinted 1993, 1994, 1997, 1998, 2000, 2003, 2009 (twice), 2012 (D)

ISBN 978 9980 58856 2

Written by Pat Lilburn, Pam Rawson and Peter Sullivan
Writing consultants Elsie Kinavai and Kate Deutrom
Papua New Guinea project co-ordinator and
writing consultant Katherine Schneider
Cover photograph by Rocky Roe Photographics
Photographs (p55) by Papua New Guinea Sports Commission
Illustrated by Annie Vanston and Mary Ann Hurley
Typeset by Solo Typesetting, South Australia
Printed and bound in Australia by Ligare Book Printers, Pty Ltd

Secretary's Message

This pupil's book is part of a new Mathematics Program designed and written for use during the early years of schooling in Papua New Guinea. The core materials consist of two pupil books called **Community School Mathematics 3A** and **Community School Mathematics 3B**. They are accompanied by the **Teacher's Resource Book 3**. They will replace the MACS series now in use.

In the Community School Mathematics Program children are taught mathematics by first using real objects. Later, the children will use pictures of objects. Finally, the children will use number symbols to represent these objects. Each school will be supplied with a set of **base ten blocks** to use during mathematics lessons. You and your pupils must also collect other real objects such as seeds, nuts, shells etc. **Always allow your pupils to use real objects during their mathematics lessons if they want to. The children will decide when they do not need the help of real objects any longer**. Remember, when children use real objects, they will understand mathematics better.

This program also encourages the children to solve their own problems and make their own decisions with confidence. In order to learn these skills, the children should talk about what they are doing in every lesson. **Since learning is most effective when it has meaning and is enjoyable, allow the children to use the language that they are most comfortable with**. However, in Grade 3, the main language of instruction should be English, with other languages including the vernacular, used to aid understanding of new and difficult concepts.

Finally, the National Department of Education wants teachers to be **flexible** in programming and timetabling. This book will show you some ways to do this.

J. E. Tetaga OBE
Secretary for Education

Contents

Unit 3 *Graphs and Place Value*

Unit 4 *Addition and Length*

Unit 5 *Subtraction and Time*

Unit 6 *Time and Fractions*

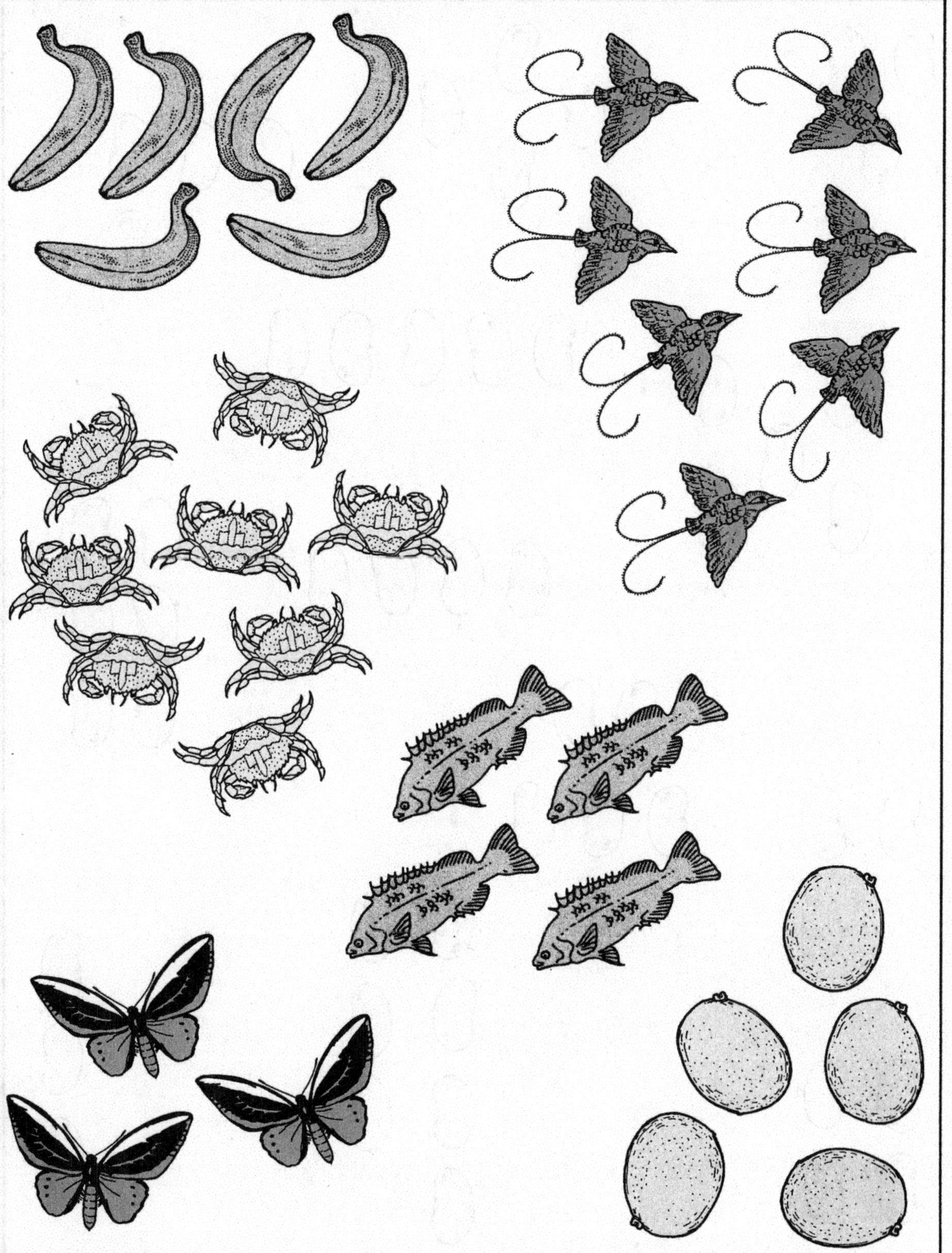

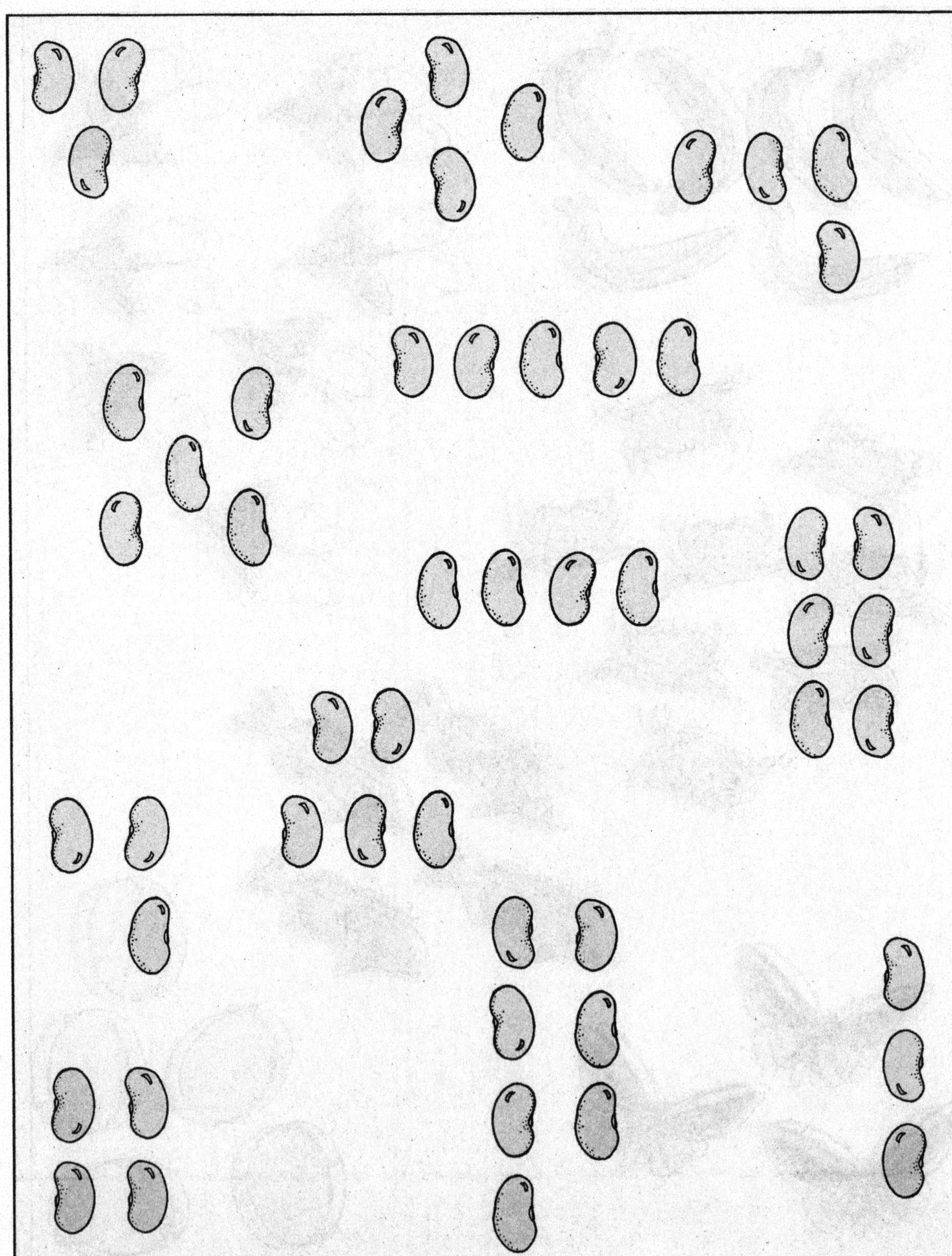

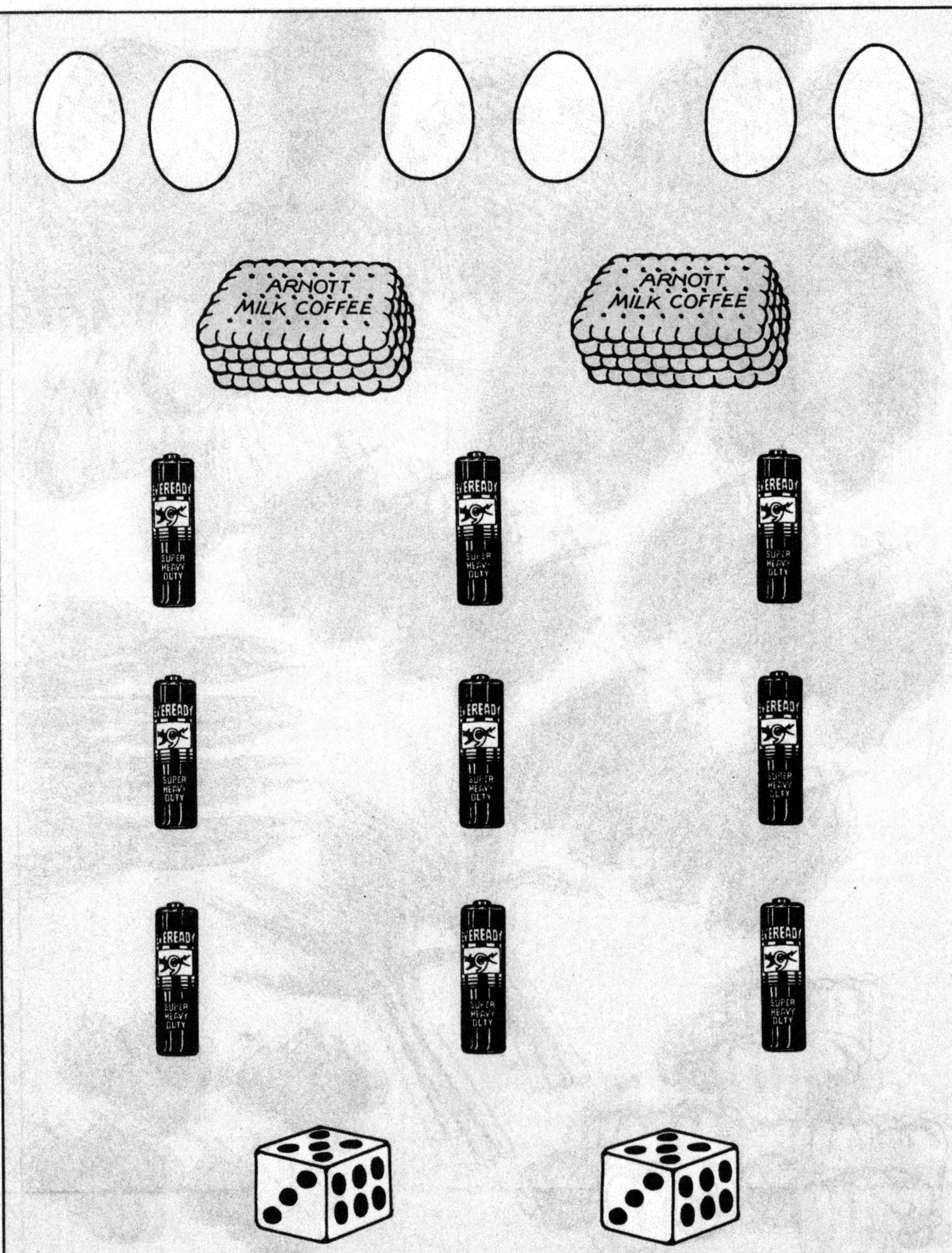
ARNOTT MILK COFFEE
ARNOTT MILK COFFEE

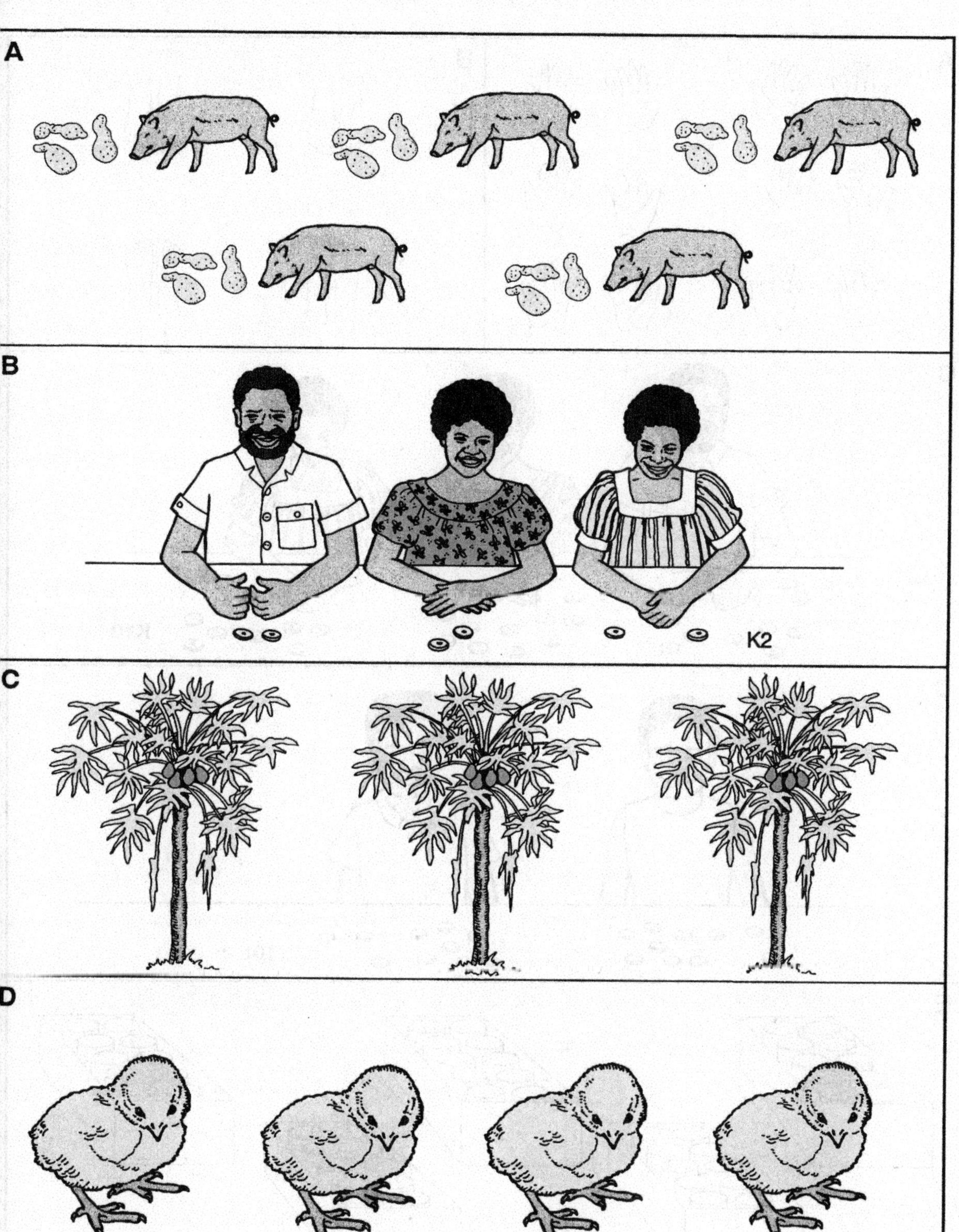
A
B
K2
C
D

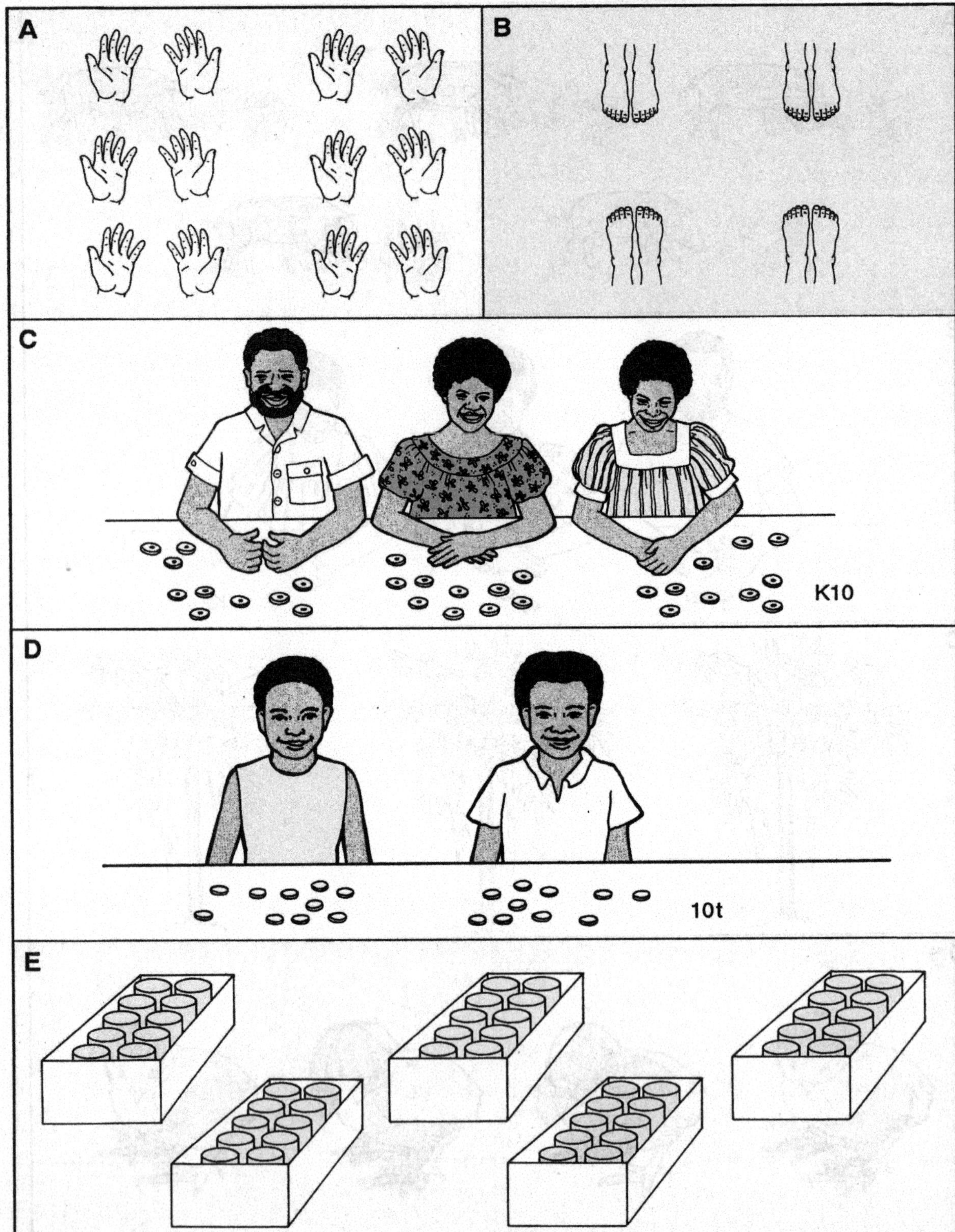
A
B
C
K10
D
10t
E

0	1	2	3	4	5	6	7	8	9
10	11	12	13	14	15	16	17	18	19
20	21	22	23	24	25	26	27	28	29
30	31	32	33	34	35	36	37	38	39
40	41	42	43	44	45	46	47	48	49
50	51	52	53	54	55	56	57	58	59
60	61	62	63	64	65	66	67	68	69
70	71	72	73	74	75	76	77	78	79
80	81	82	83	84	85	86	87	88	89
90	91	92	93	94	95	96	97	98	99

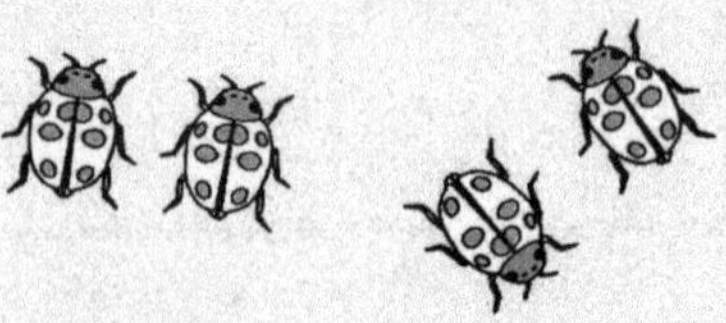

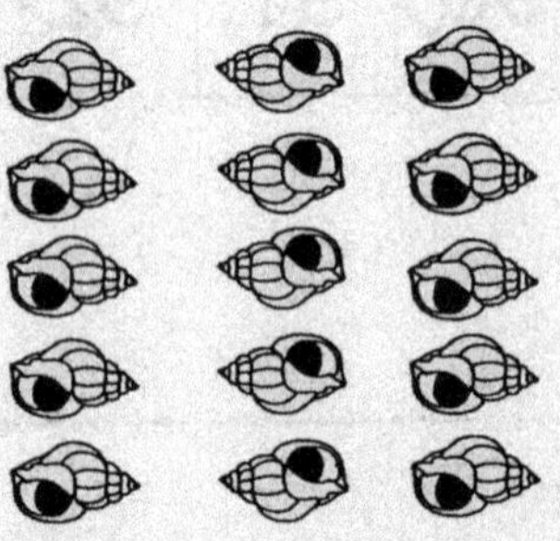

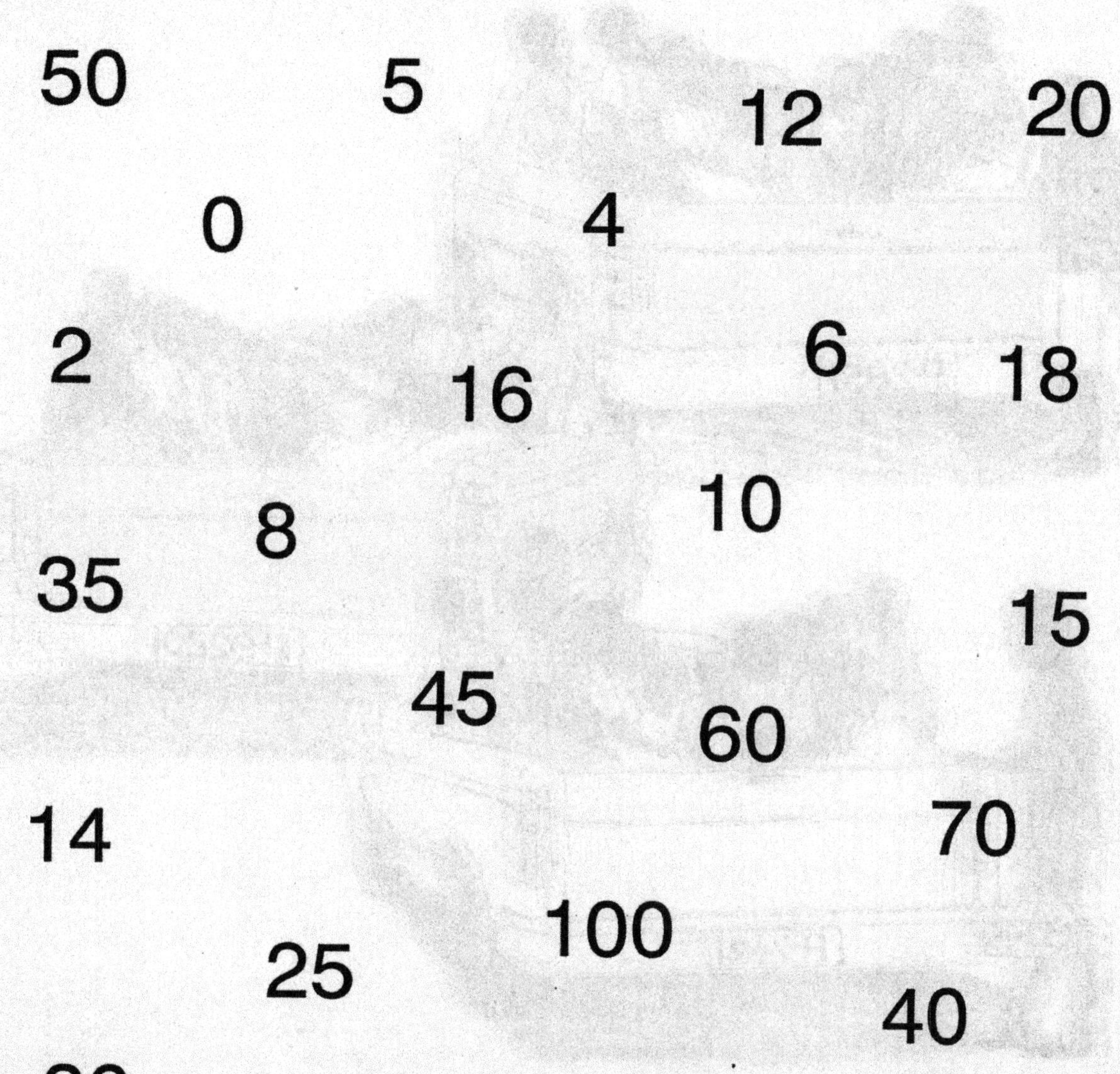

50 5 12 20

0 4

2 6 16 18

8 10

35 15

45 60

14 70

100

25 40

30

90 80

$$2 \times 5 + 1 =$$

$$3 \times 2 + 1 =$$

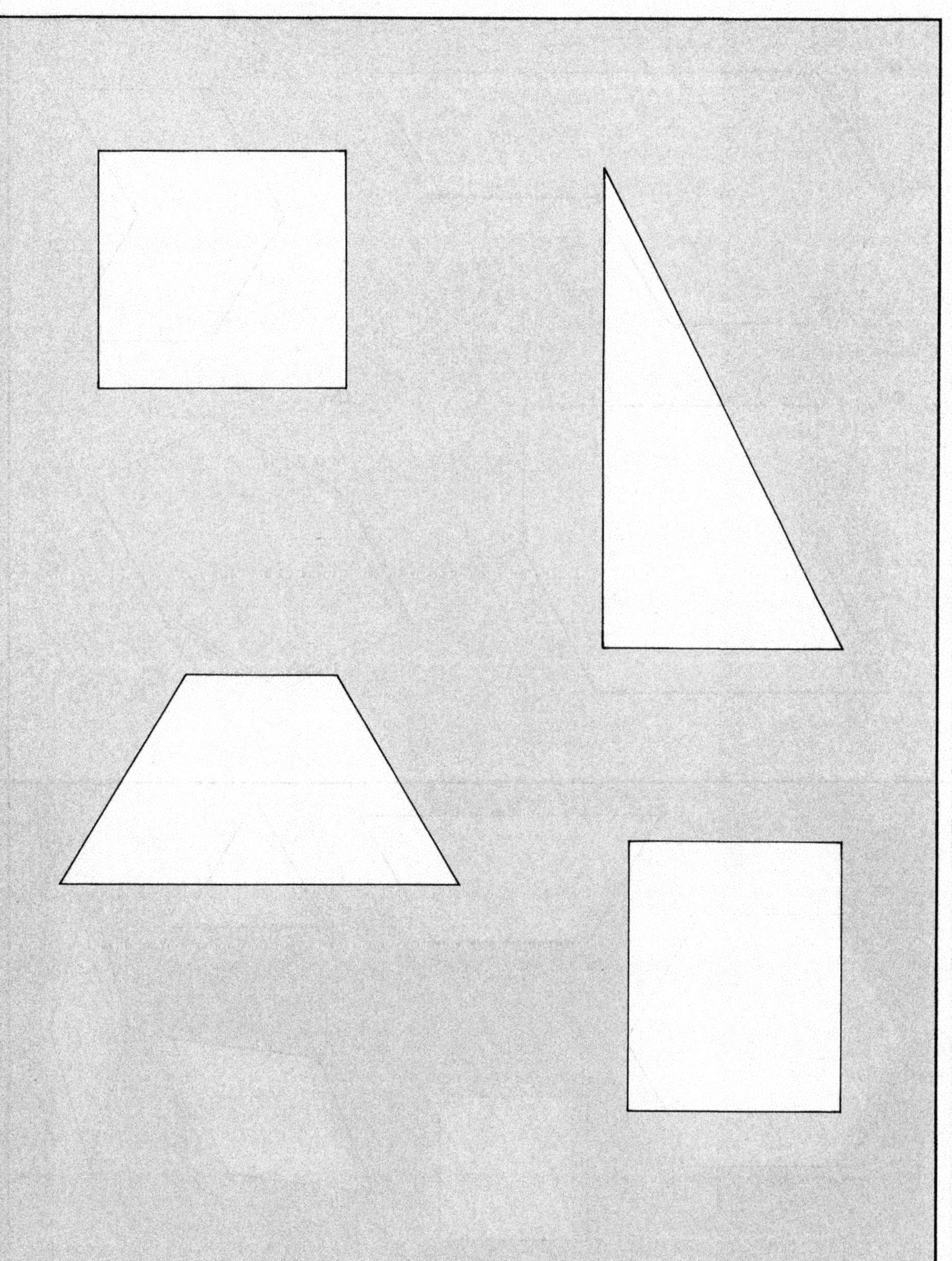

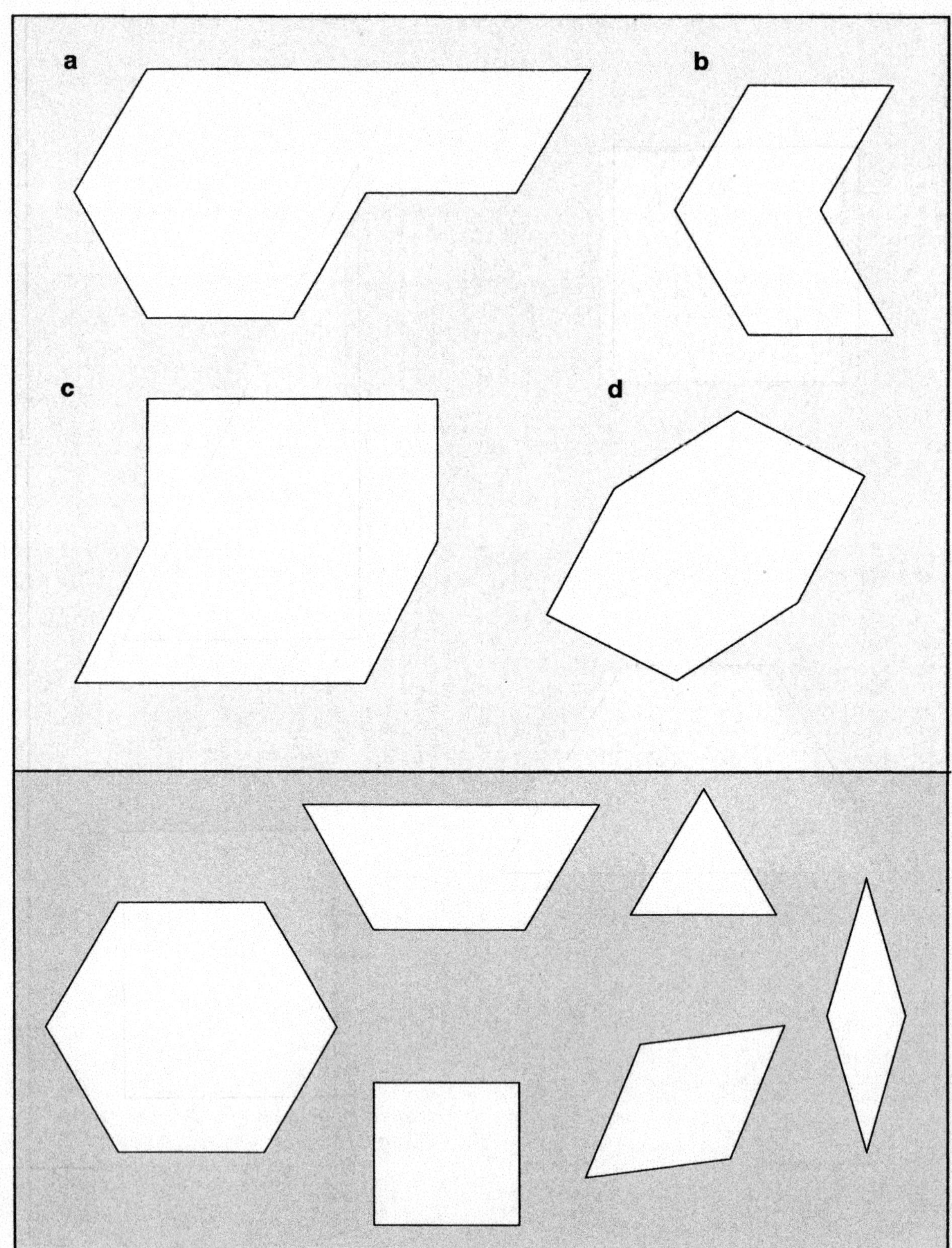
a
b
c
d

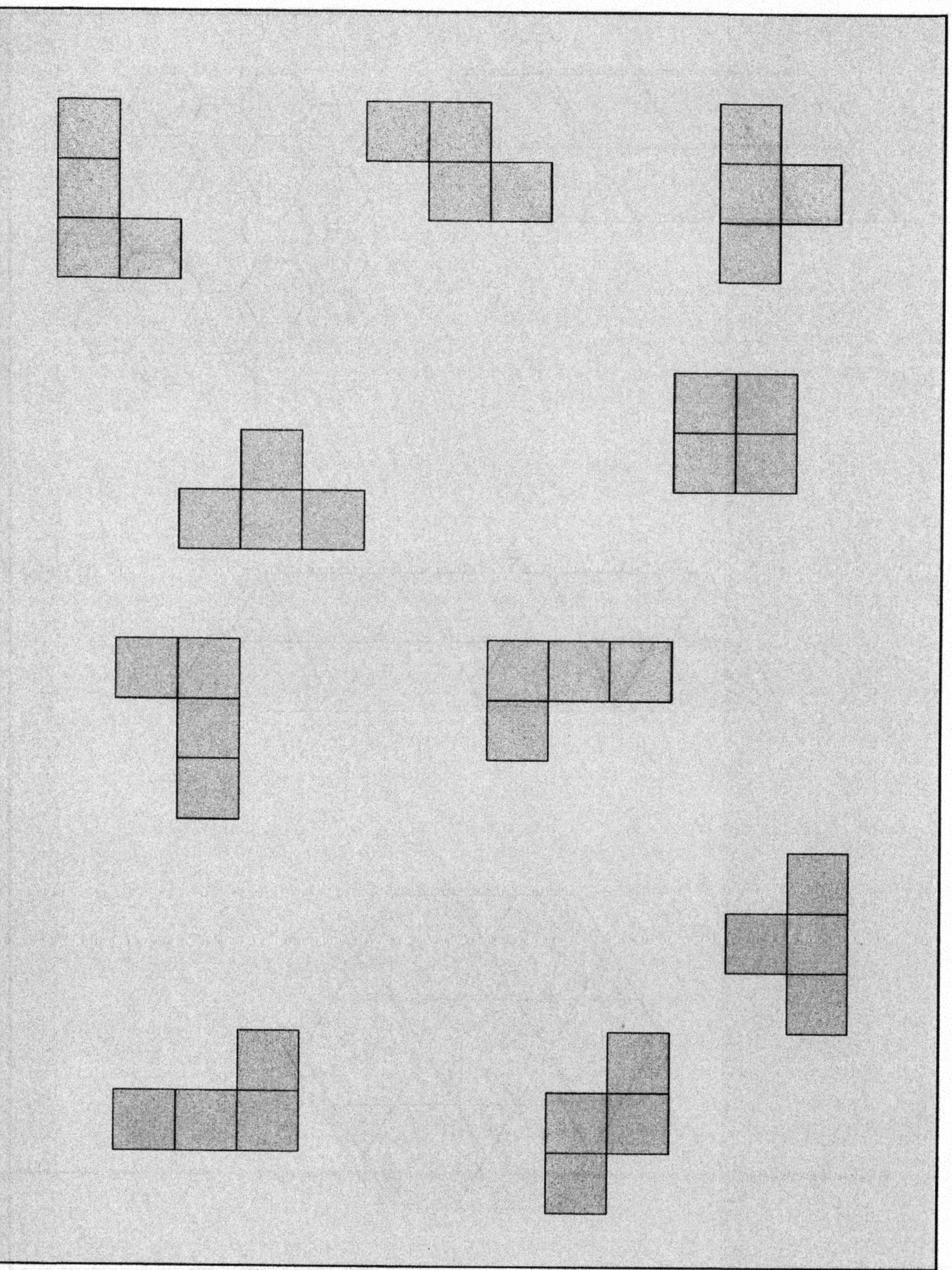

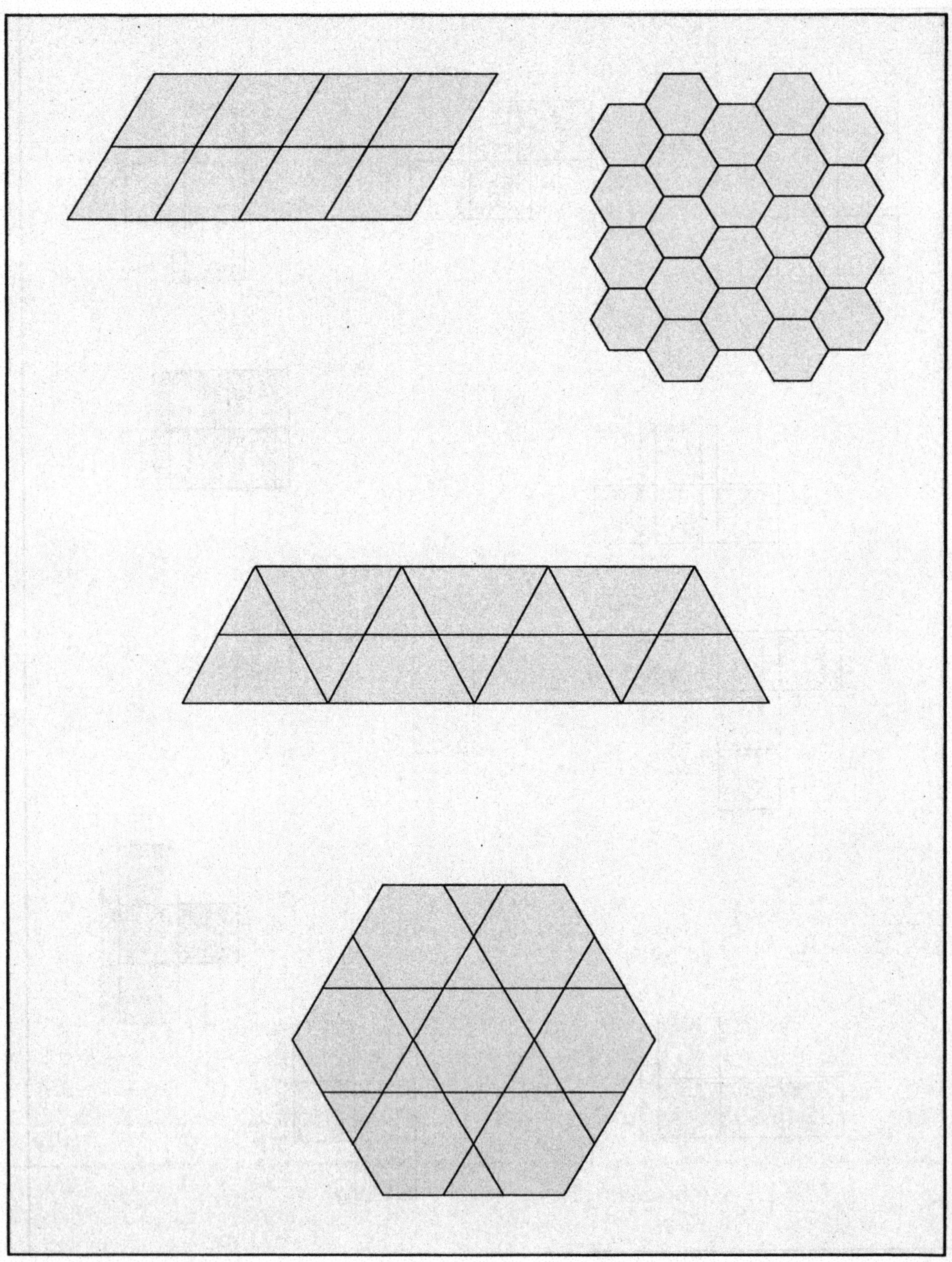

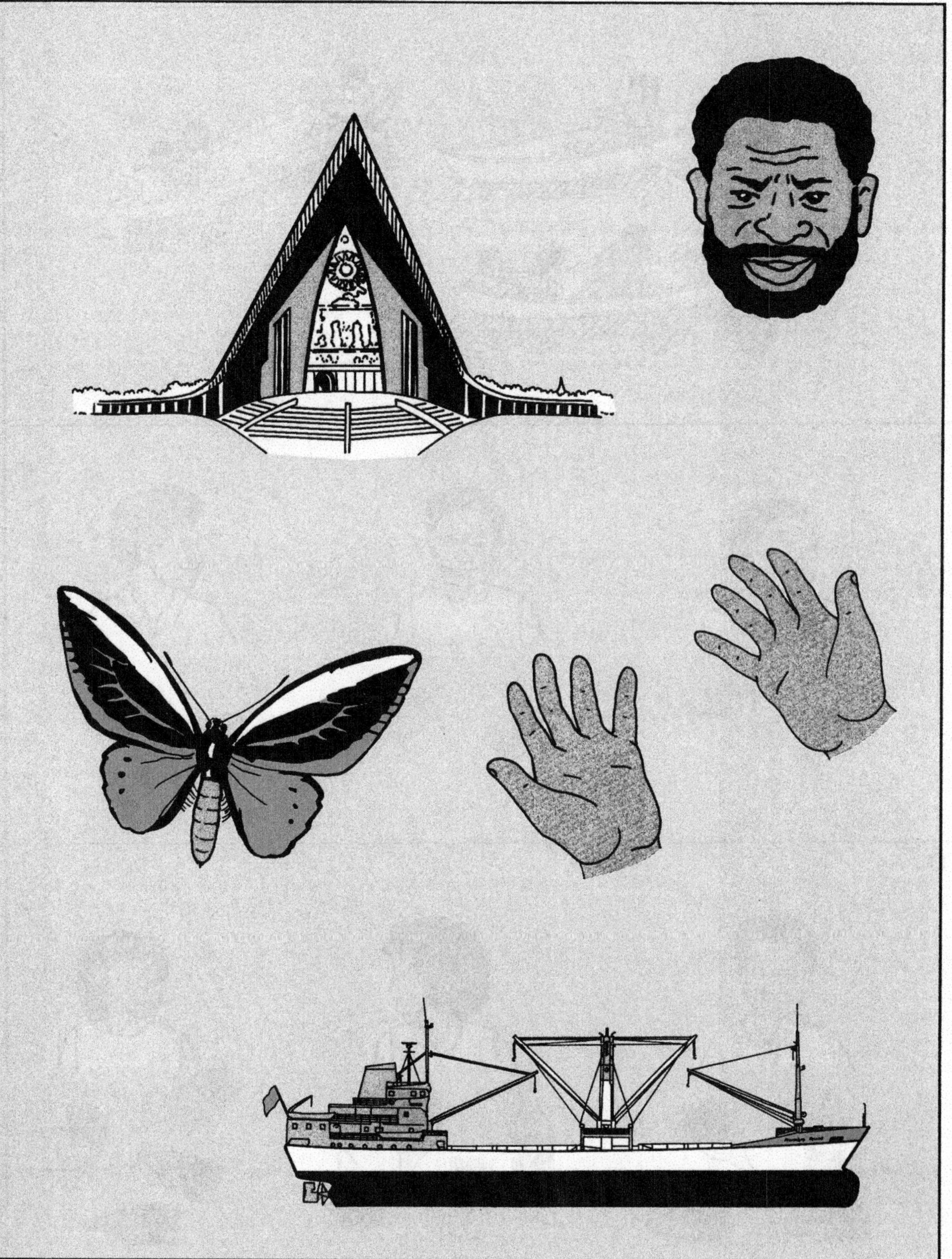

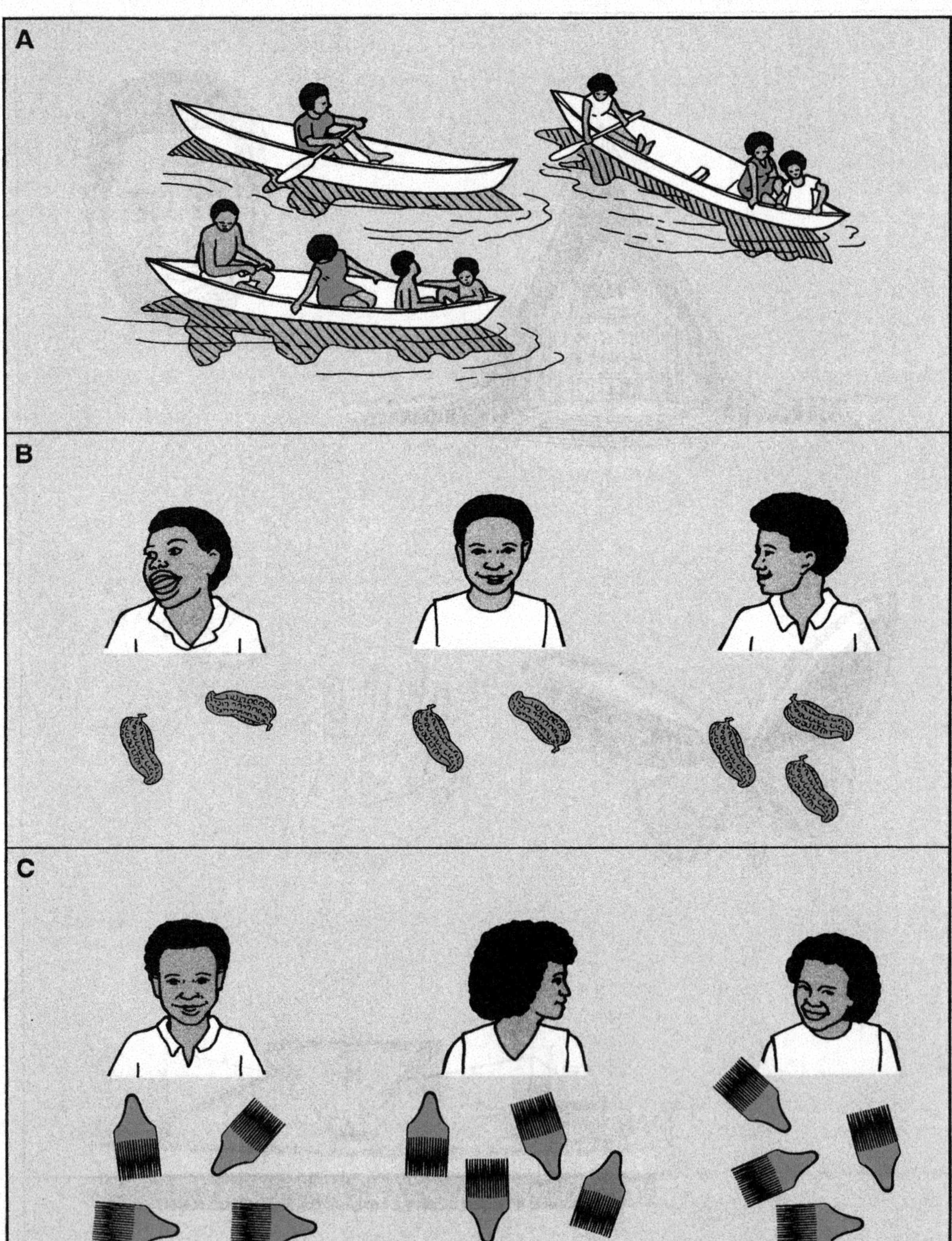
A
B
C

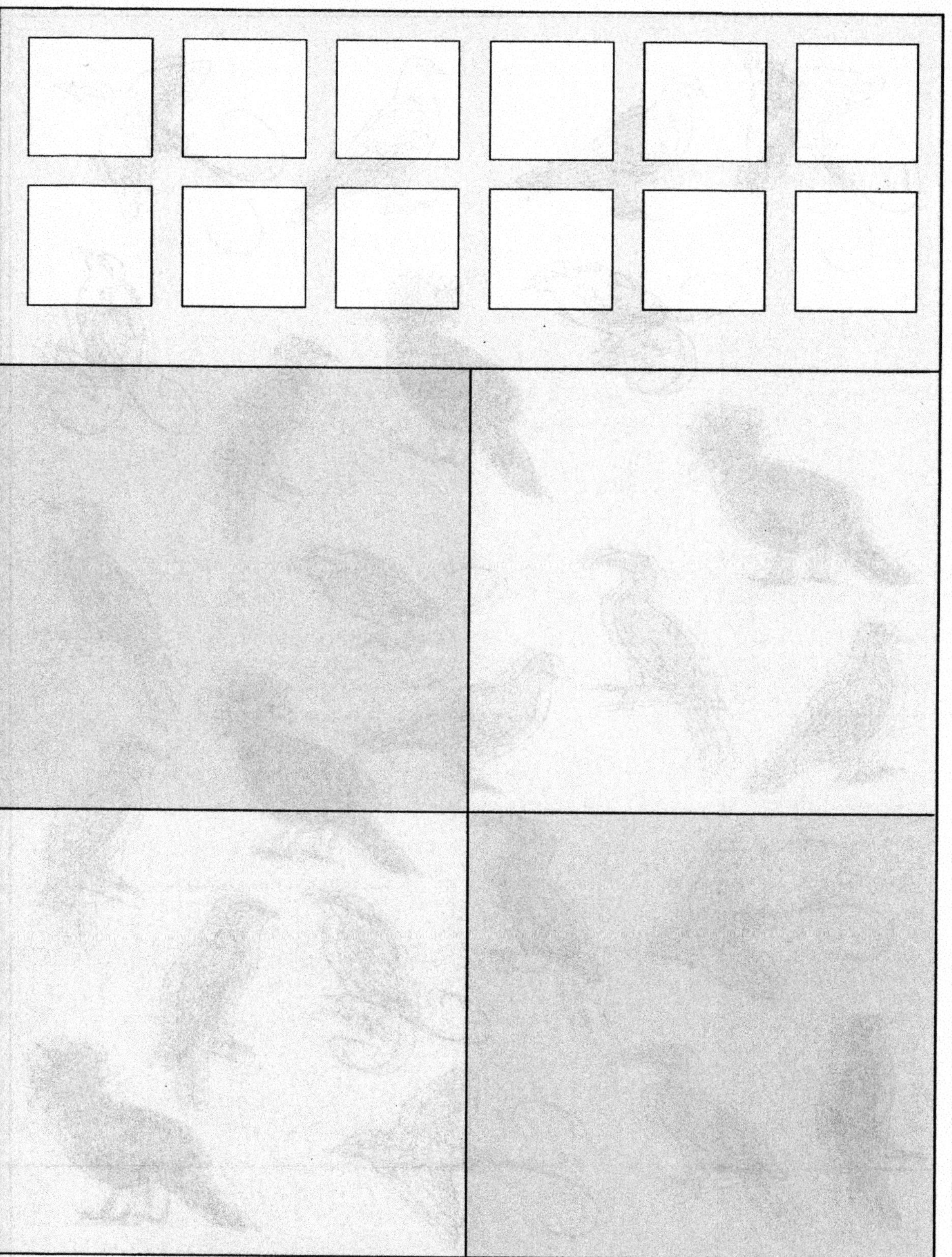

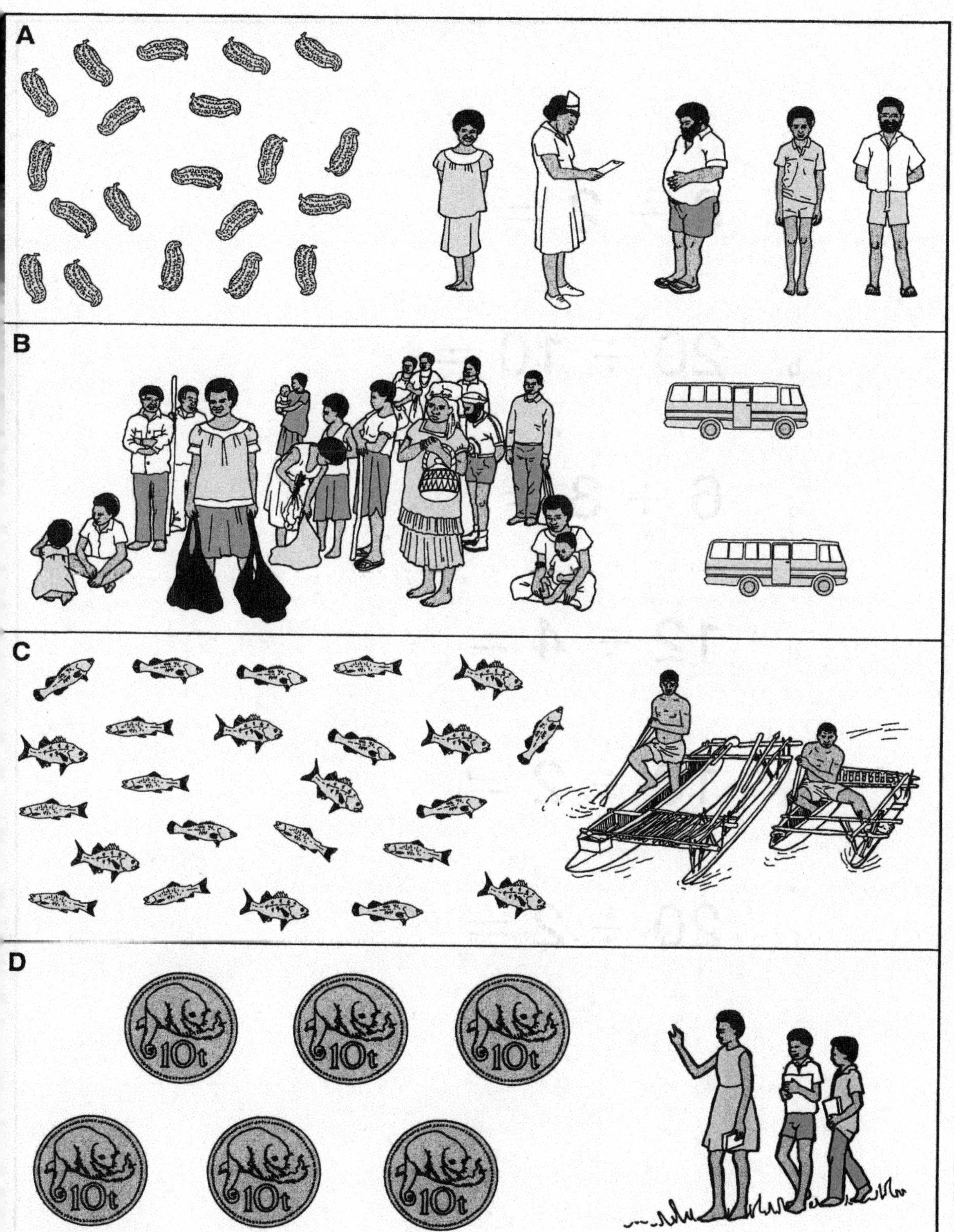
A
B
C
D
10t
10t
10t
10t
10t
10t

a $8 \div 2 =$

b $20 \div 10 =$

c $6 \div 3 =$

d $12 \div 4 =$

e $10 \div 2 =$

f $20 \div 2 =$

a $3 \times 2 = 6$

b $8 \div 2 = 4$

c $\square \div 2 = 4$

d $2 \times \square = 6$

e $6 \div \square = 2$

f $\square \div 4 = 2$

g $\square \times 4 = 8$

h $\square \div 2 = 3$

$\square \div \square = 2$

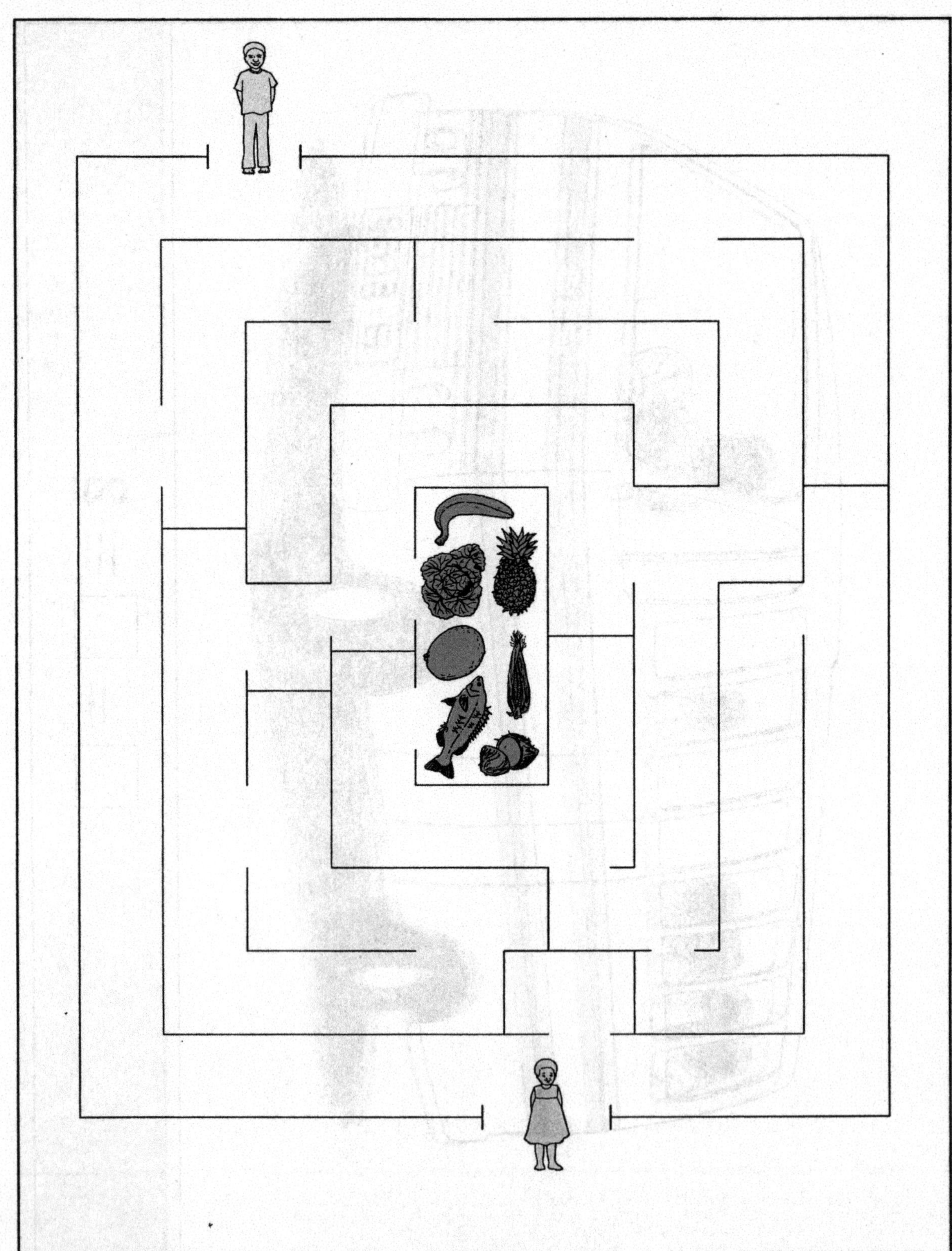

N
W
E
S

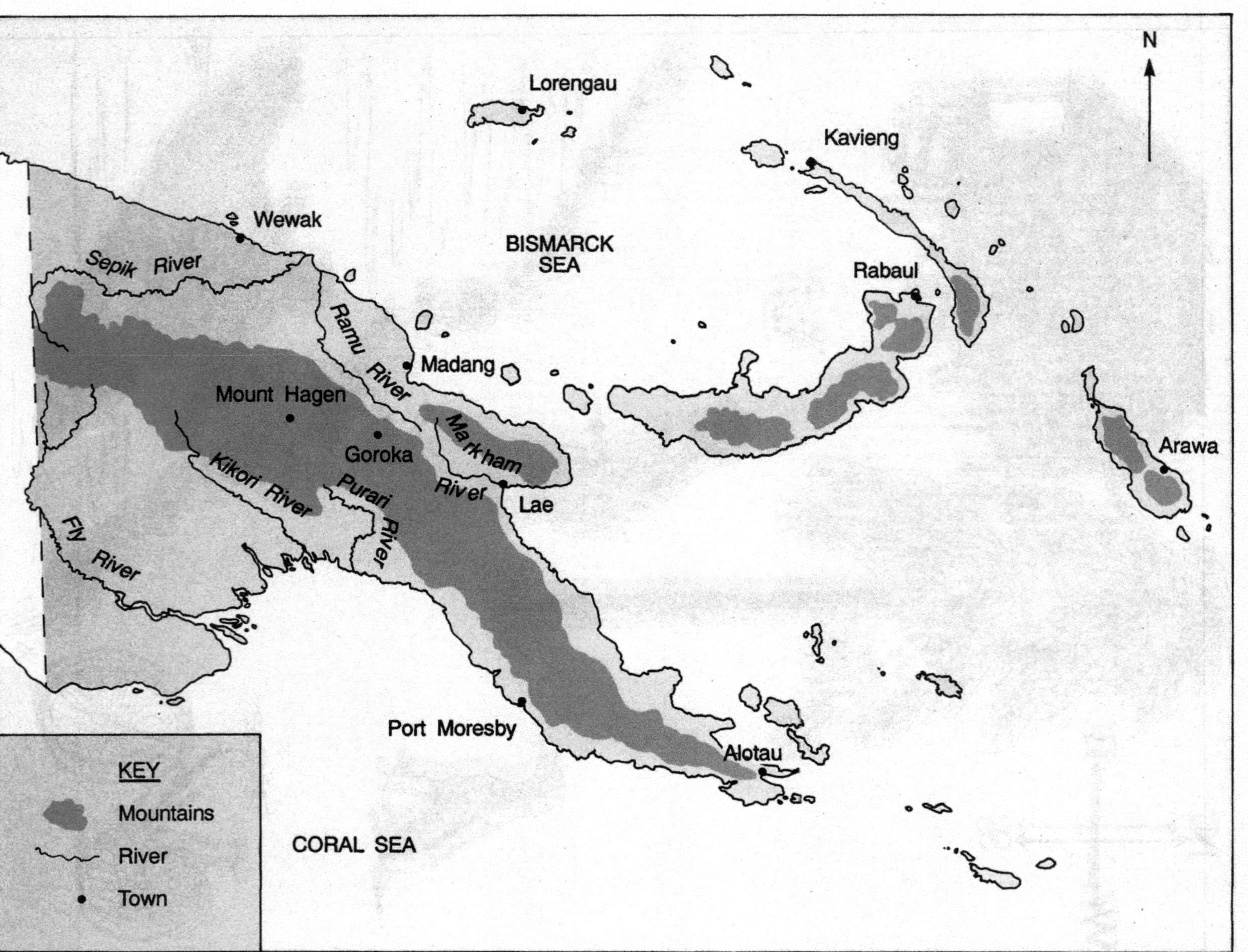
N
Lorengau
Kavieng
Wewak
BISMARCK SEA
Rabaul
Sepik River
Ramu River
Madang
Mount Hagen
Goroka
Markham River
Arawa
Kikori River
Purari River
Lae
Fly River
Port Moresby
Alotau
KEY
Mountains
River
Town
CORAL SEA

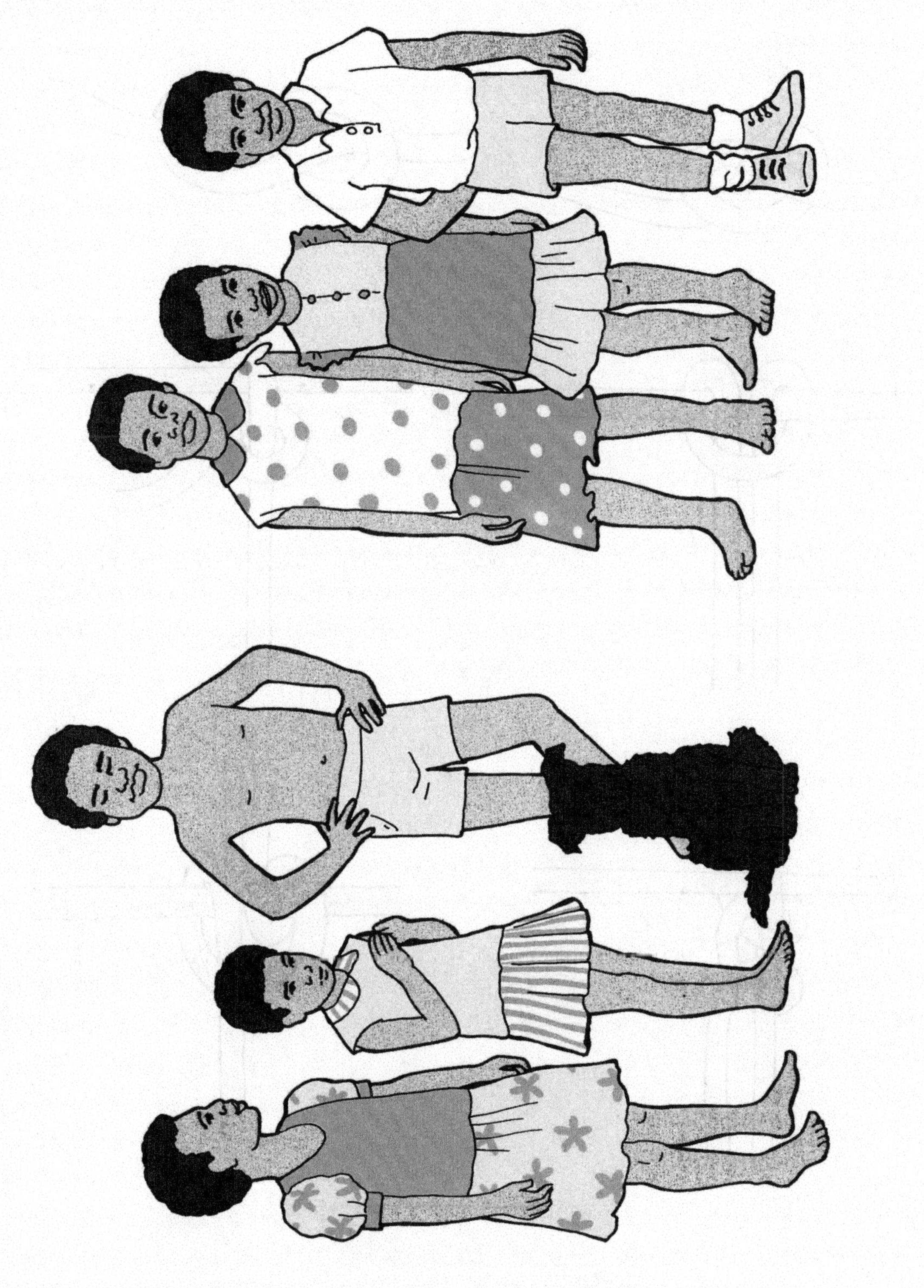

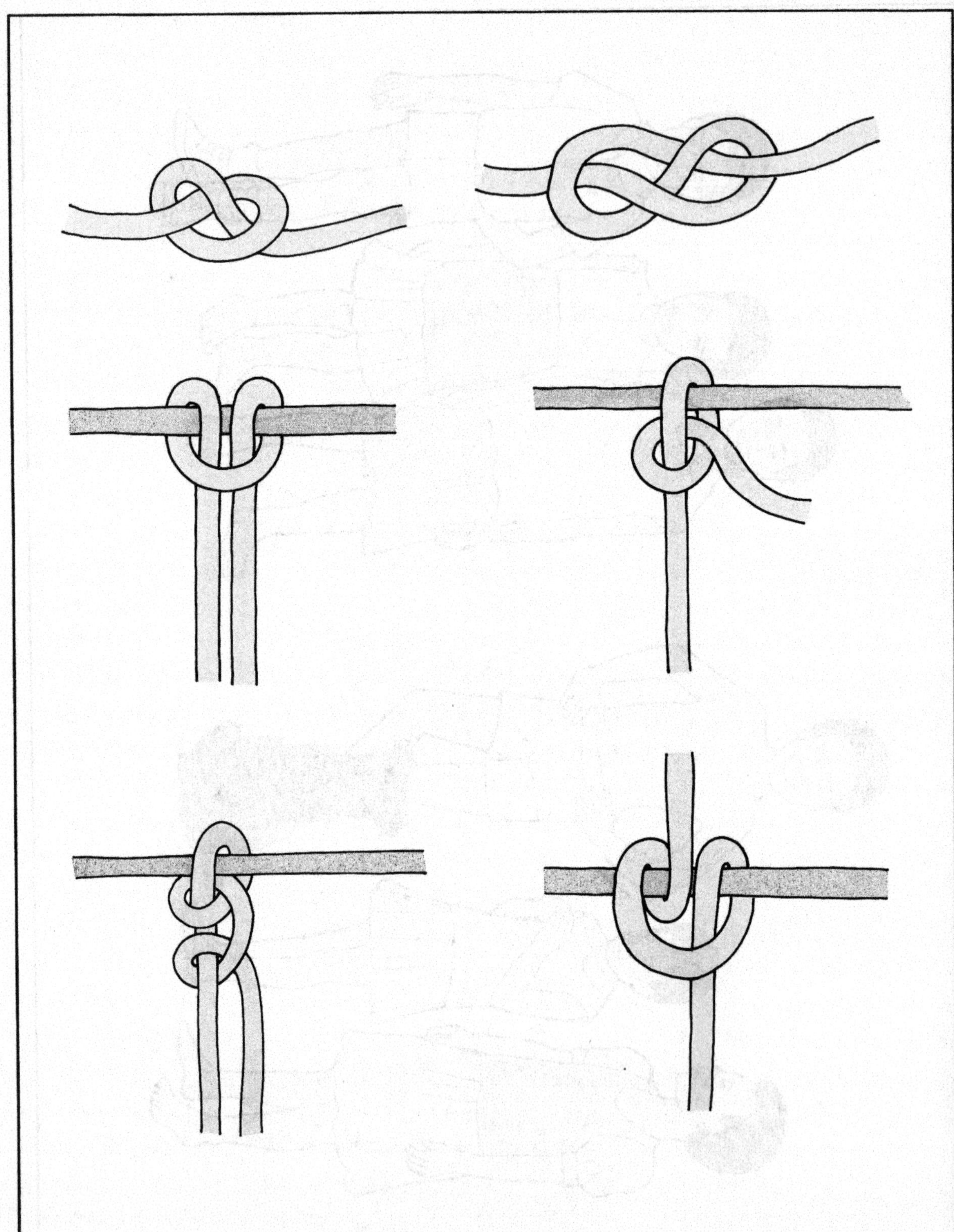

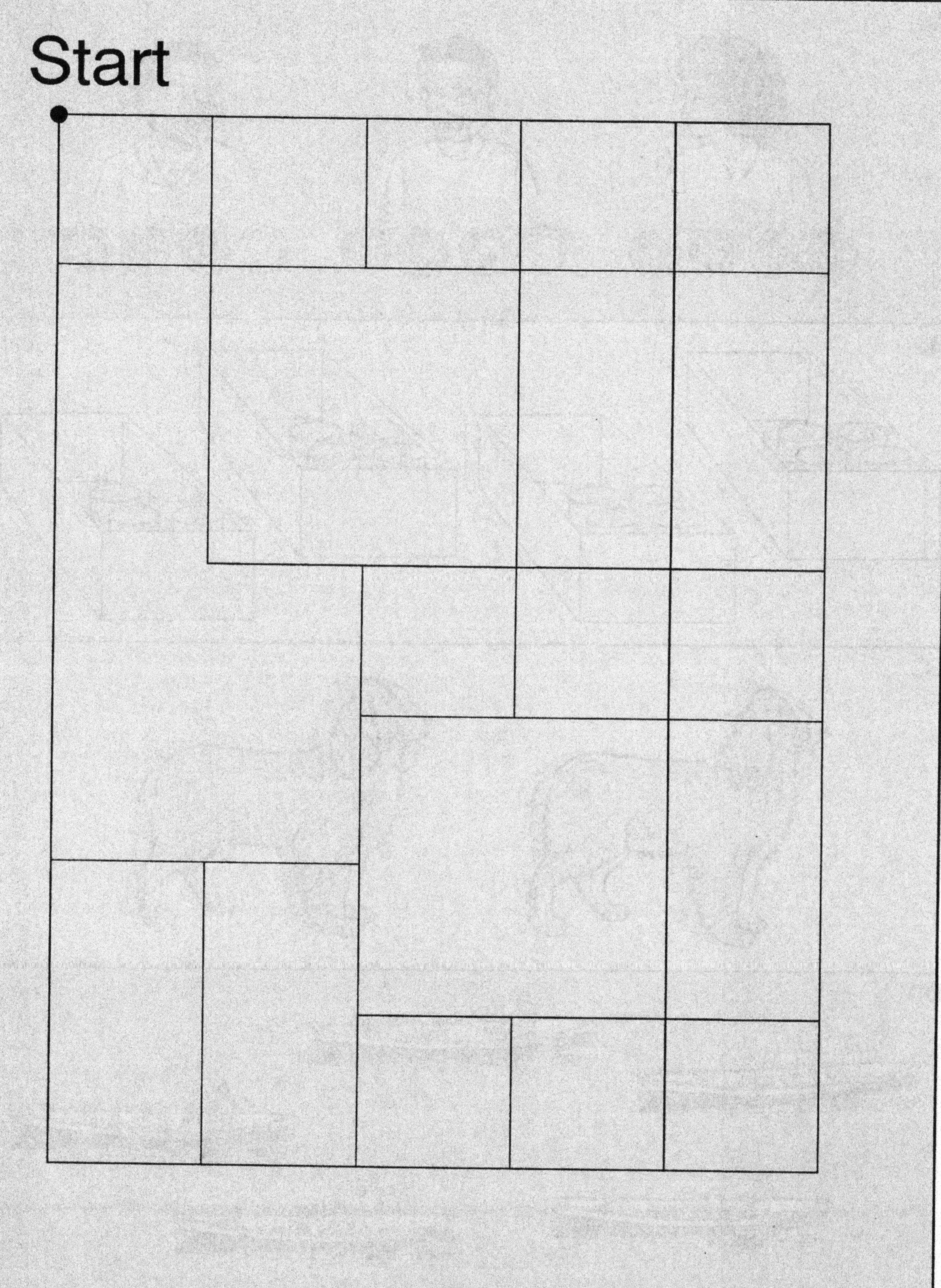
Start

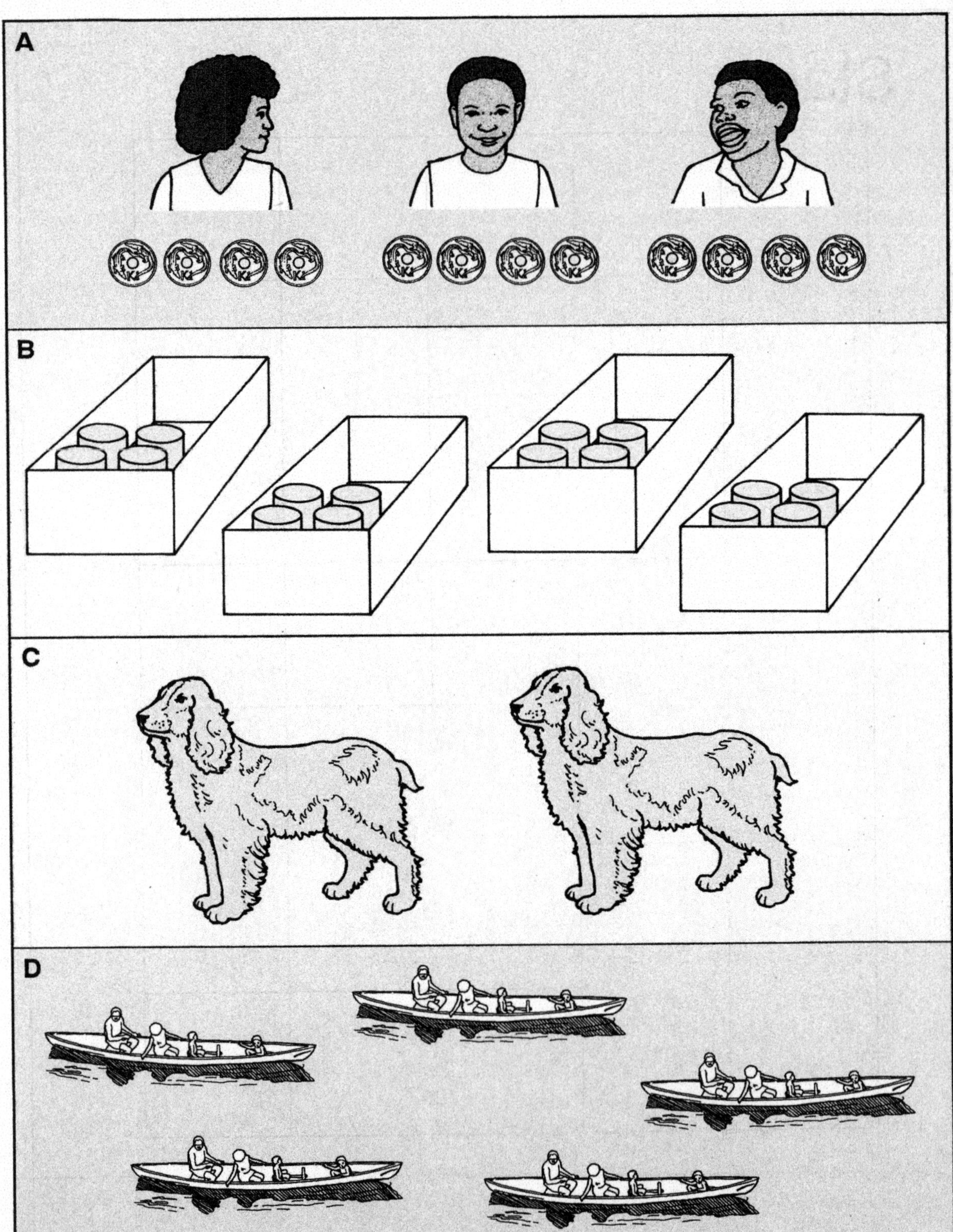
A
B
C
D

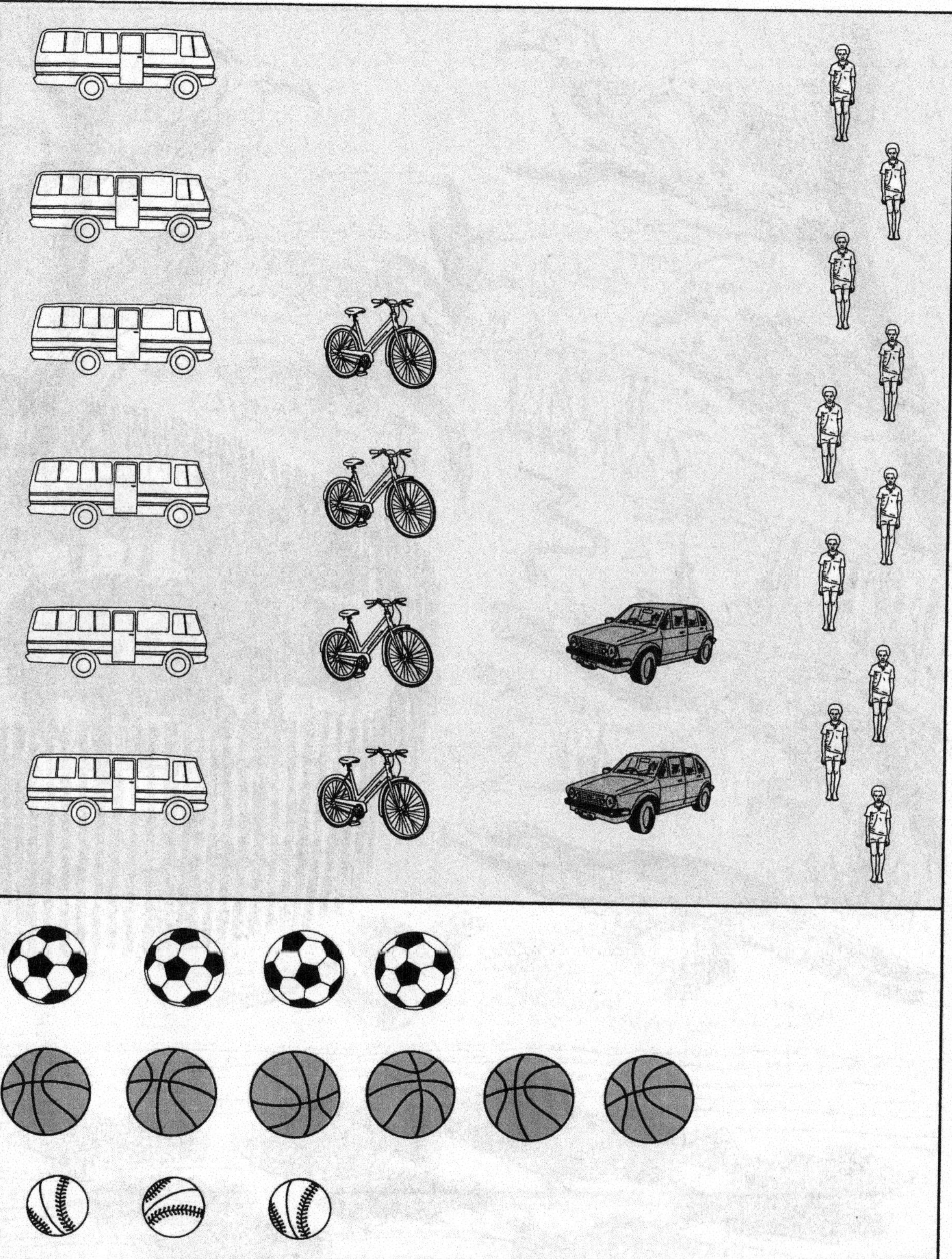

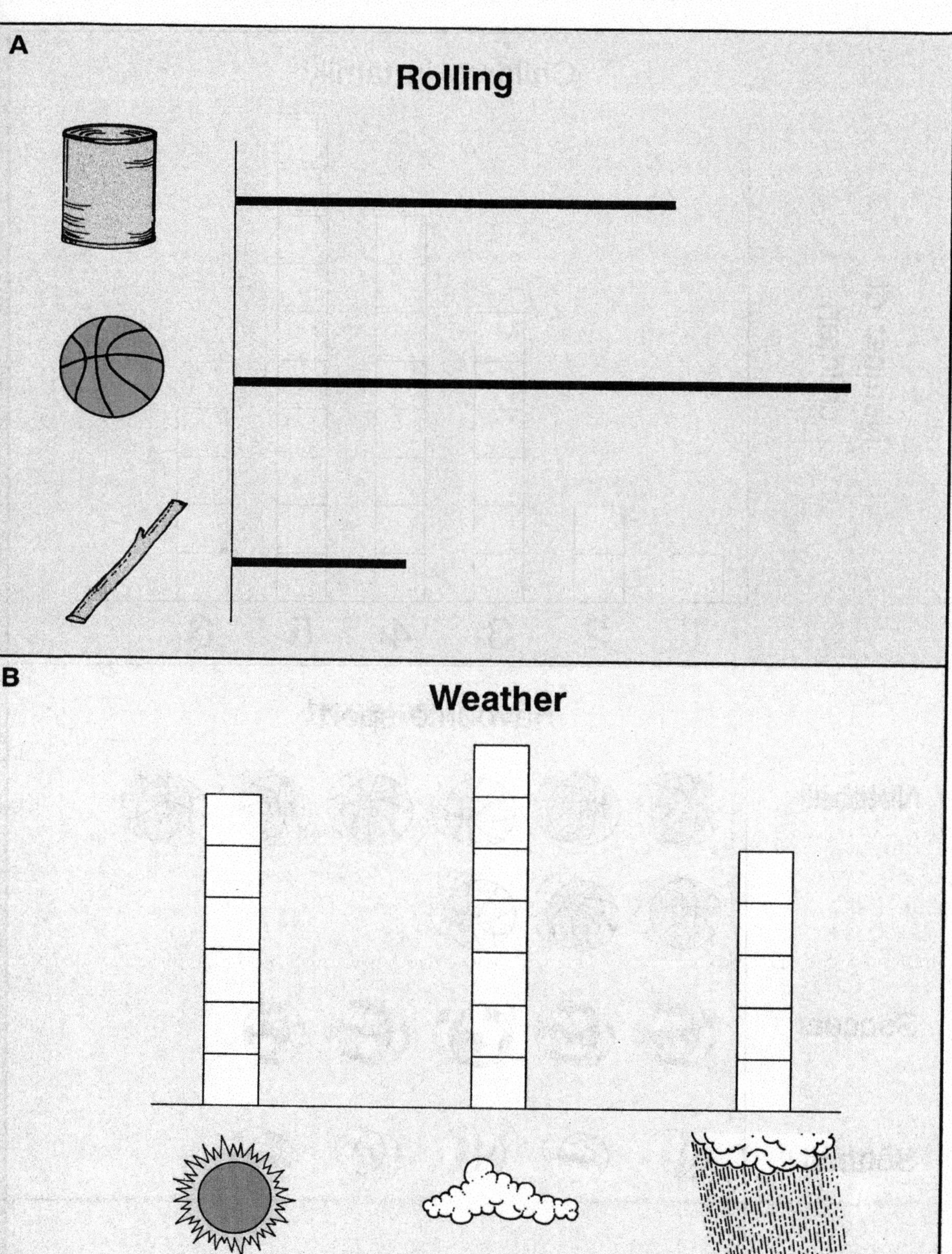
A
Rolling
B
Weather

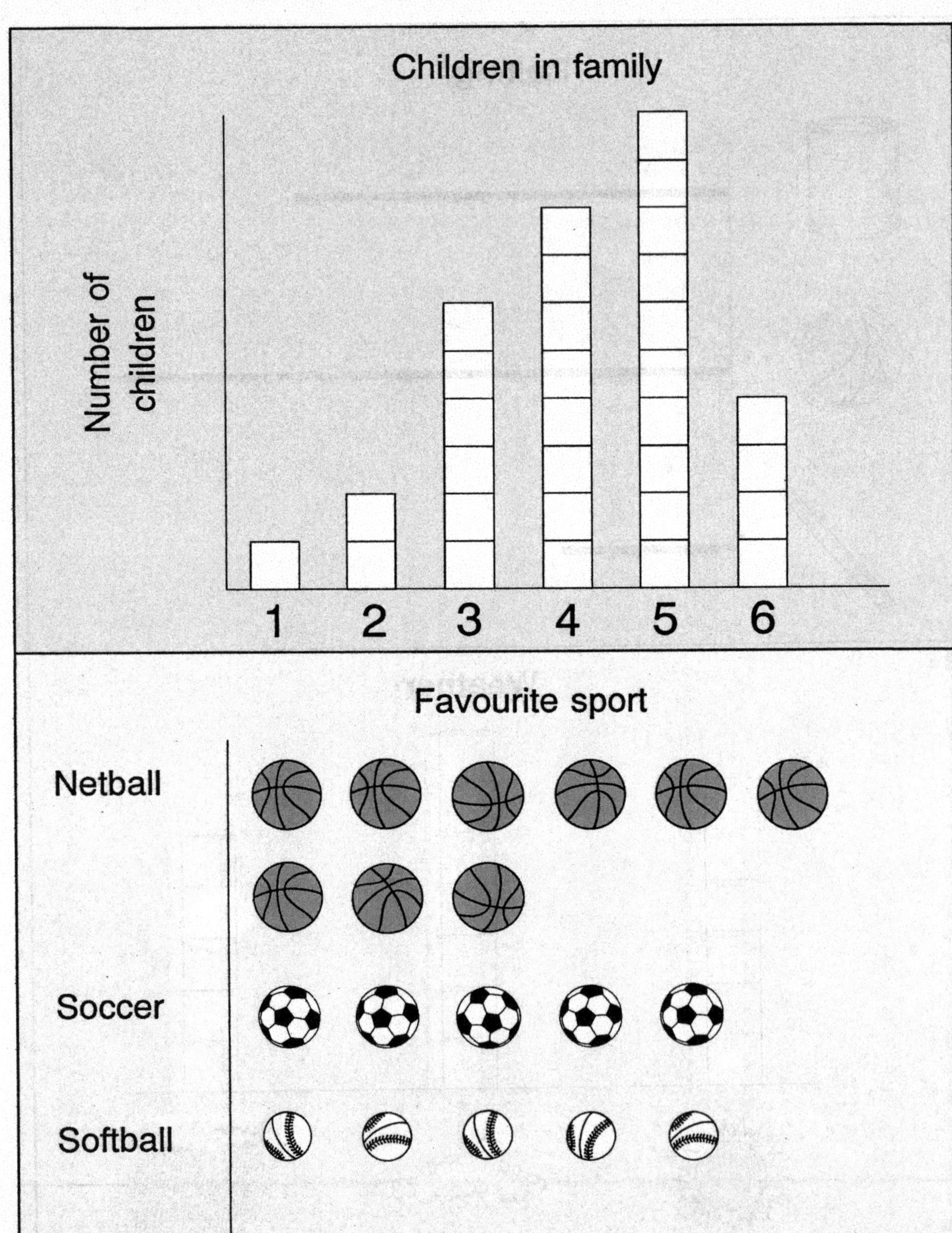
Children in family
Number of children
1
2
3
4
5
6
Favourite sport
Netball
Soccer
Softball

Once upon a time there was a small village. The village was near a mountain. A river ran at the foot of the mountain. The people in the village were unhappy. The village was full of rats. There were rats in the houses. There were rats in the school. There were rats in the gardens. There were rats everywhere!

The rats ate the food. The rats ate the clothes. They bit the people's toes. The people tried to kill the rats. There were too many. The rats liked the village. There was plenty to eat. The villagers didn't know what to do. No one could help.

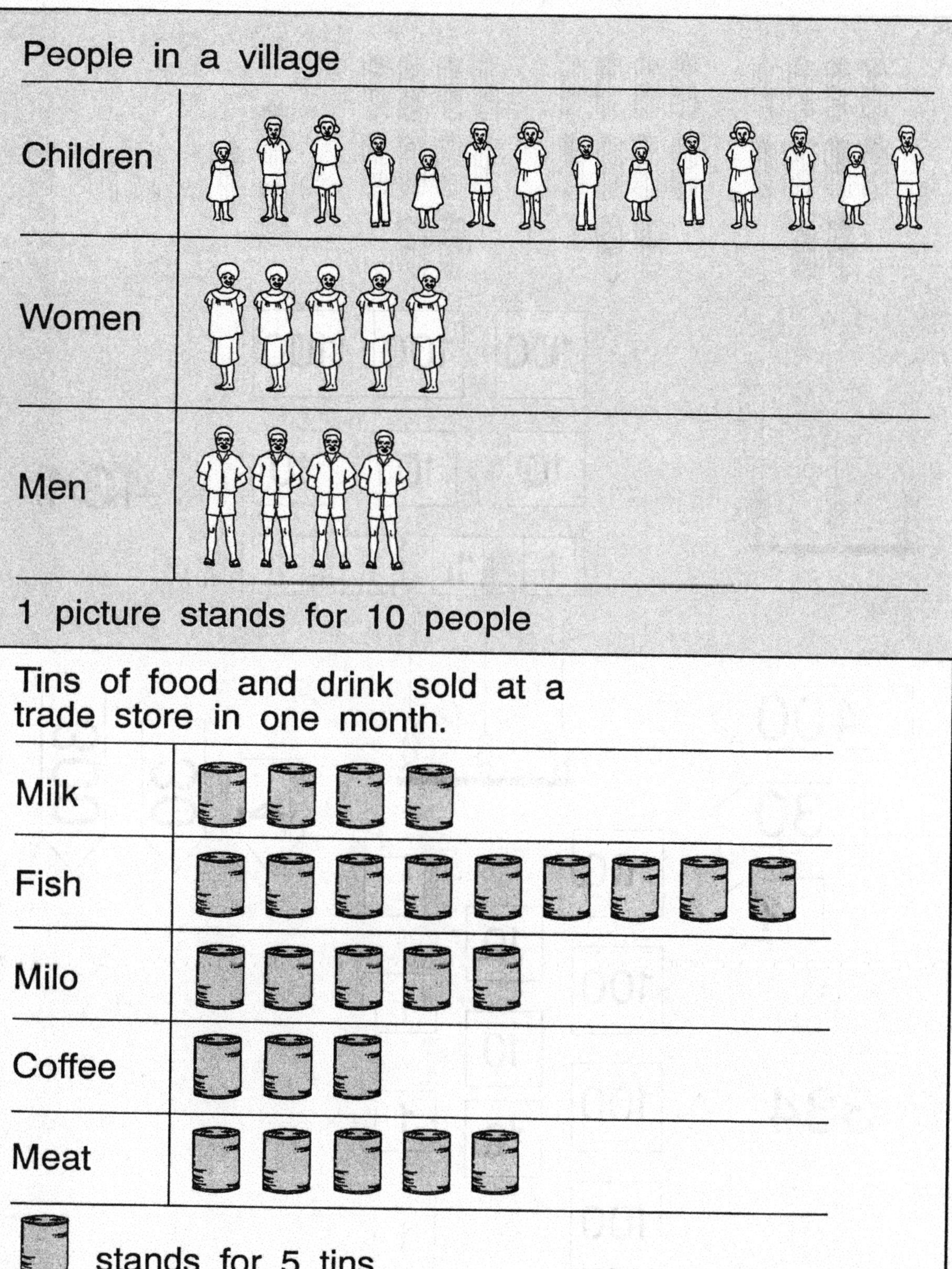
People in a village
Children
Women
Men
1 picture stands for 10 people
Tins of food and drink sold at a trade store in one month.
Milk
Fish
Milo
Coffee
Meat
stands for 5 tins

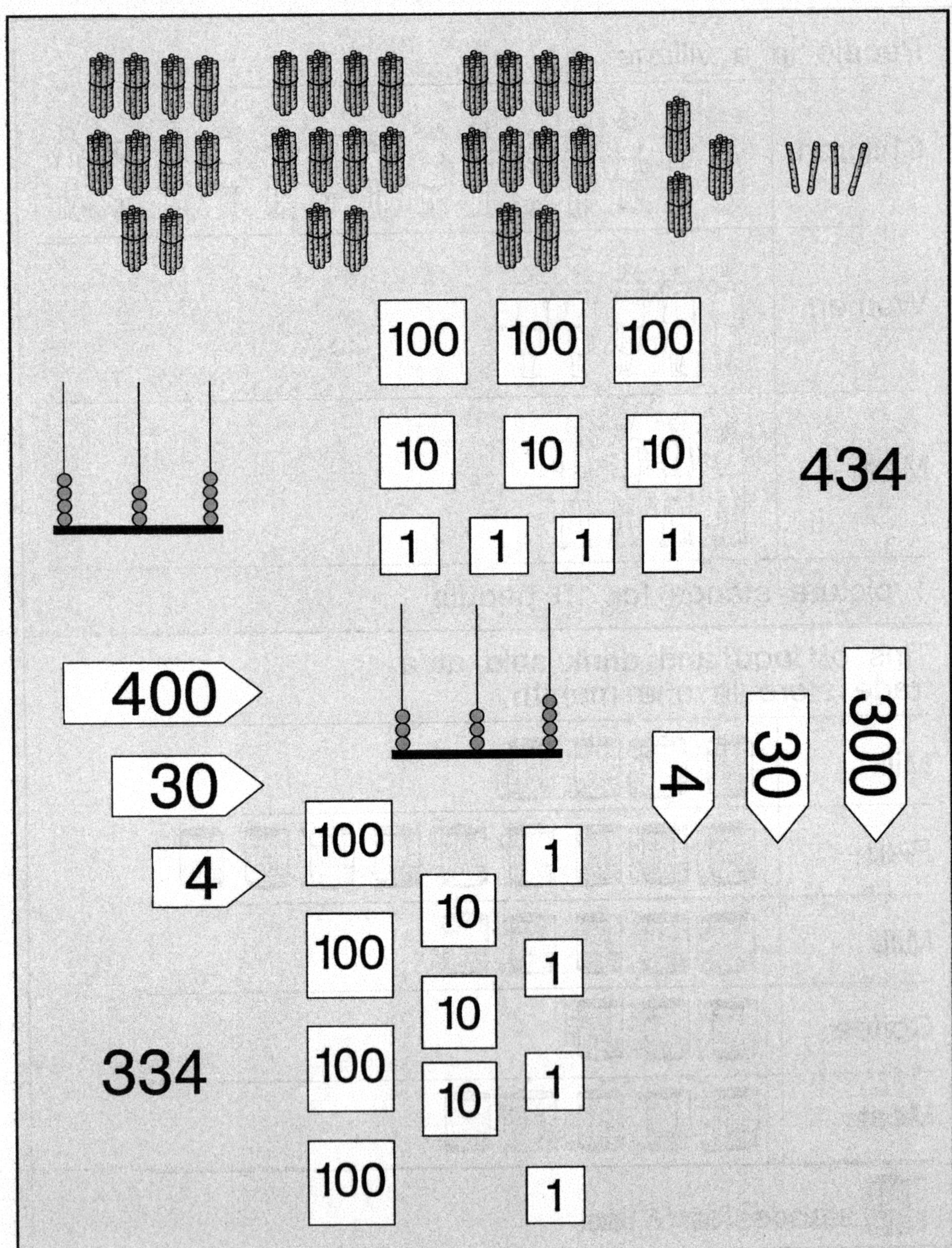
100
100
100
10
10
10
434
1
1
1
1
400
30
4
300
30
4
100
1
10
100
1
10
334
100
10
1
100
1

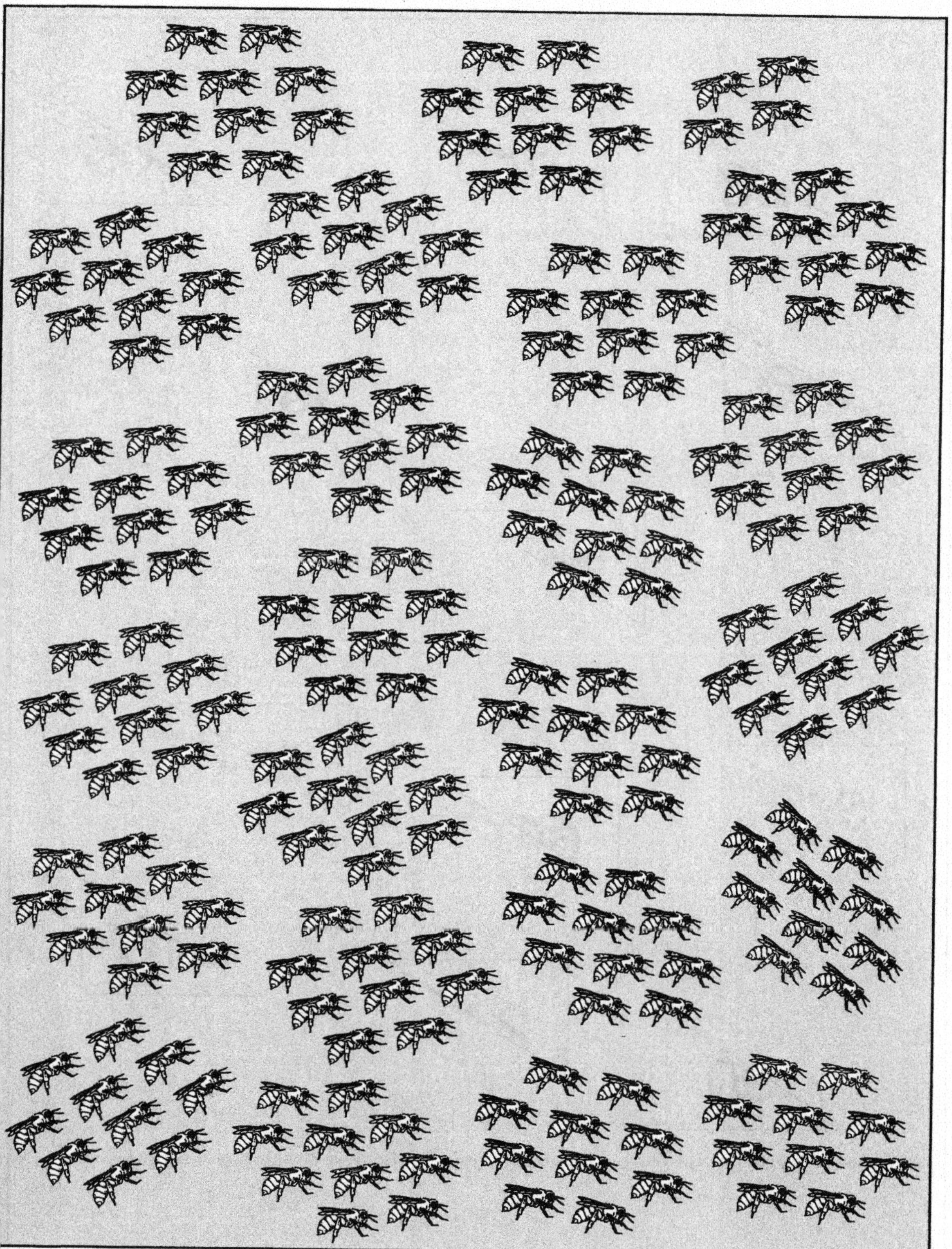

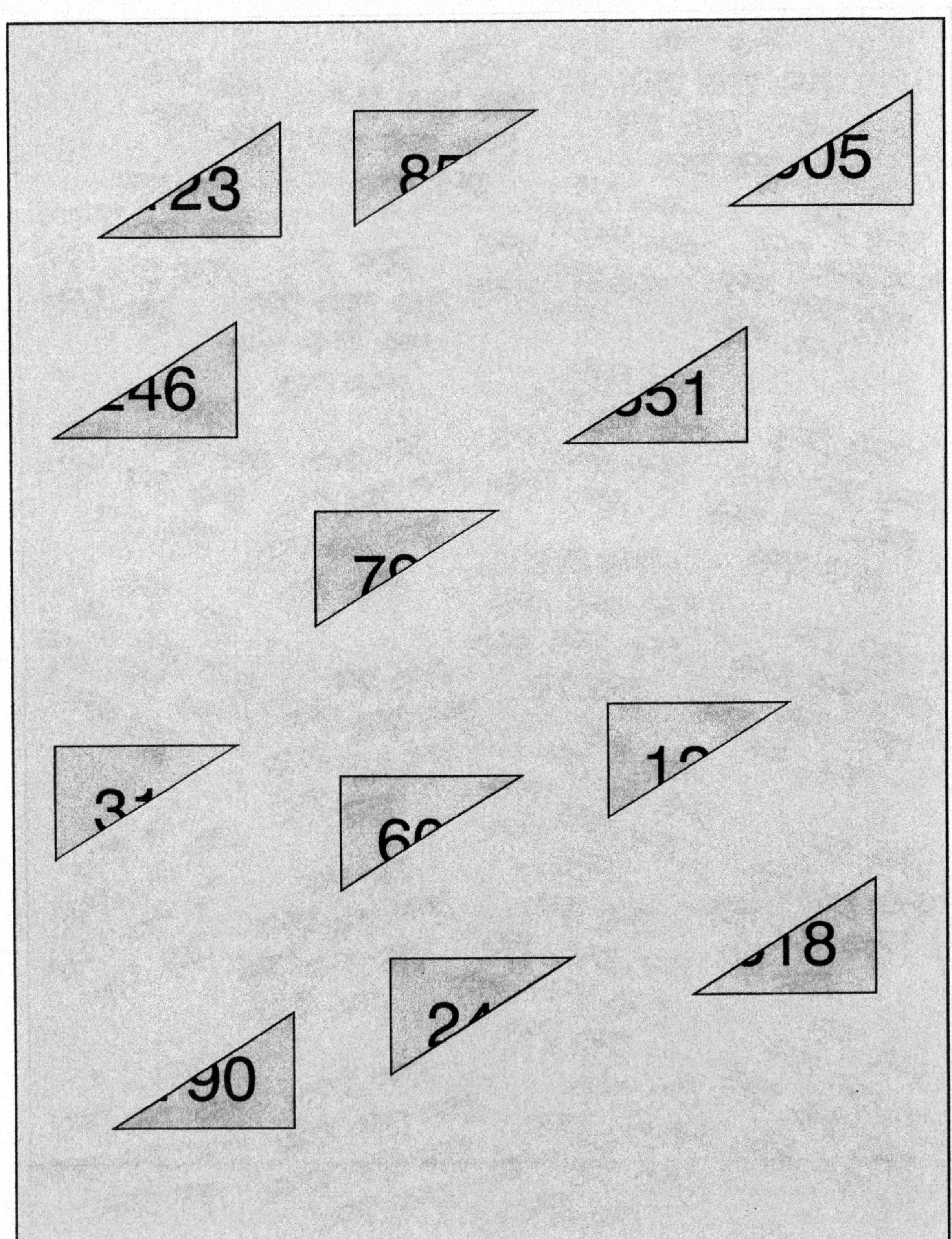

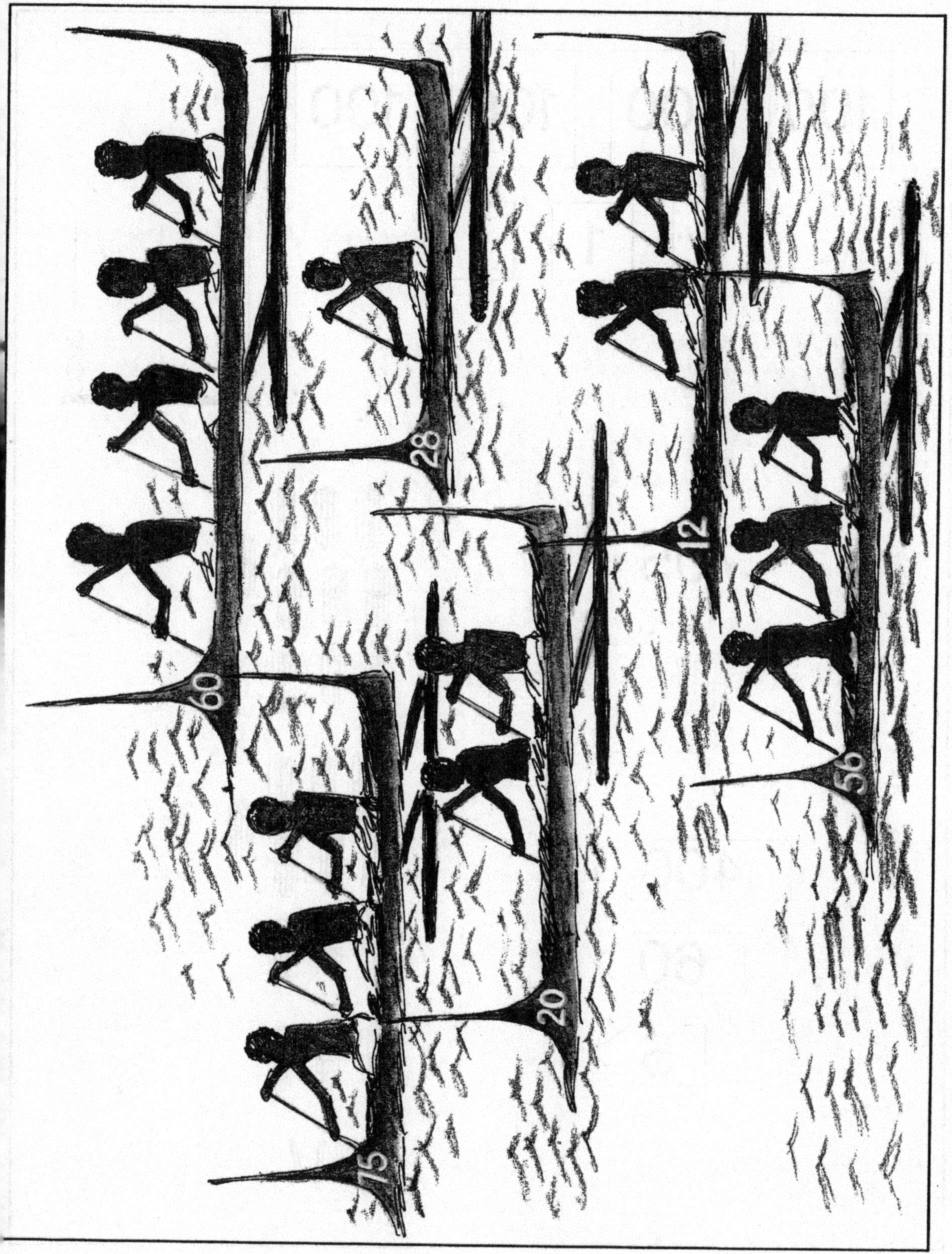
60
28
12
56
20
75

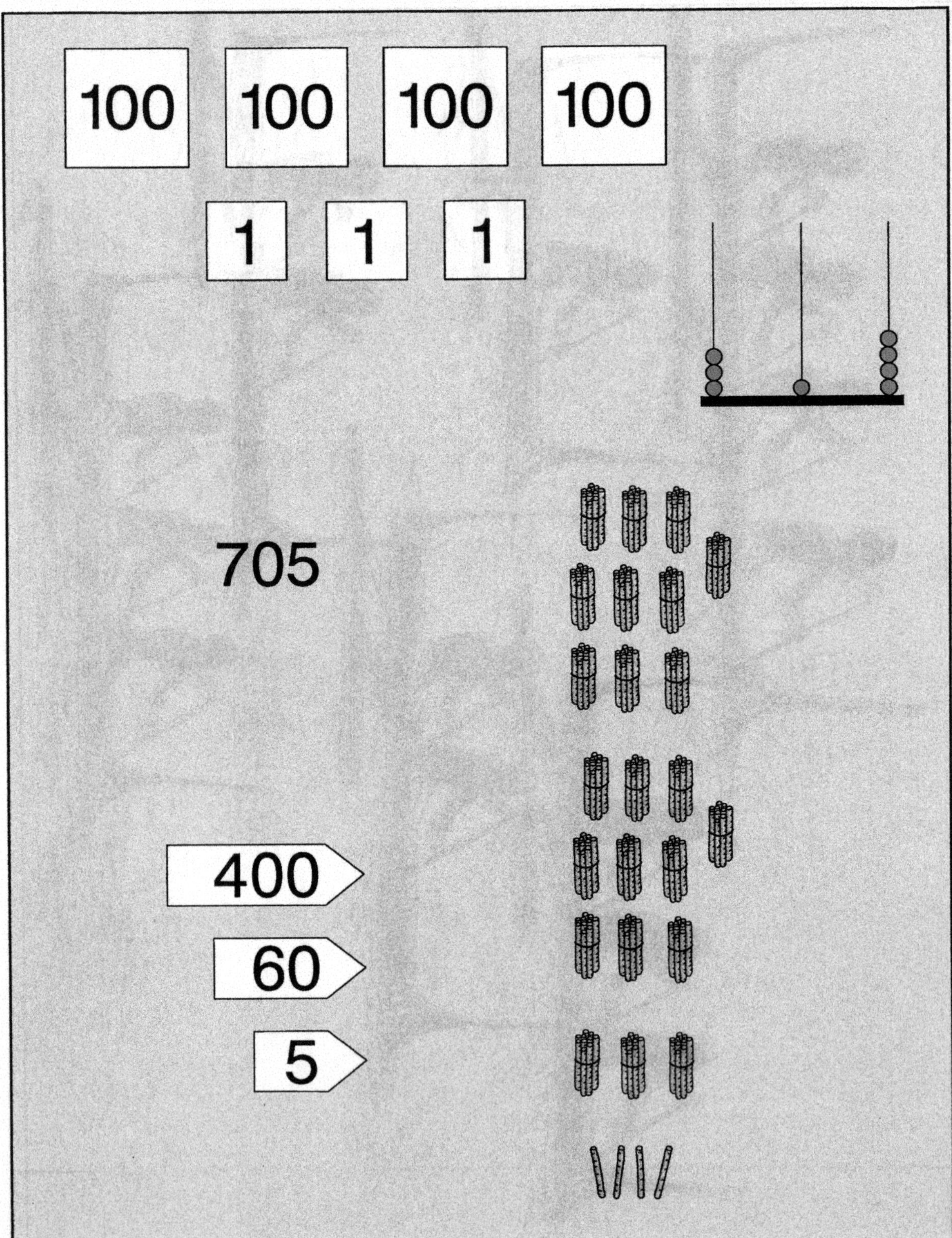
100
100
100
100
1
1
1
705
400
60
5

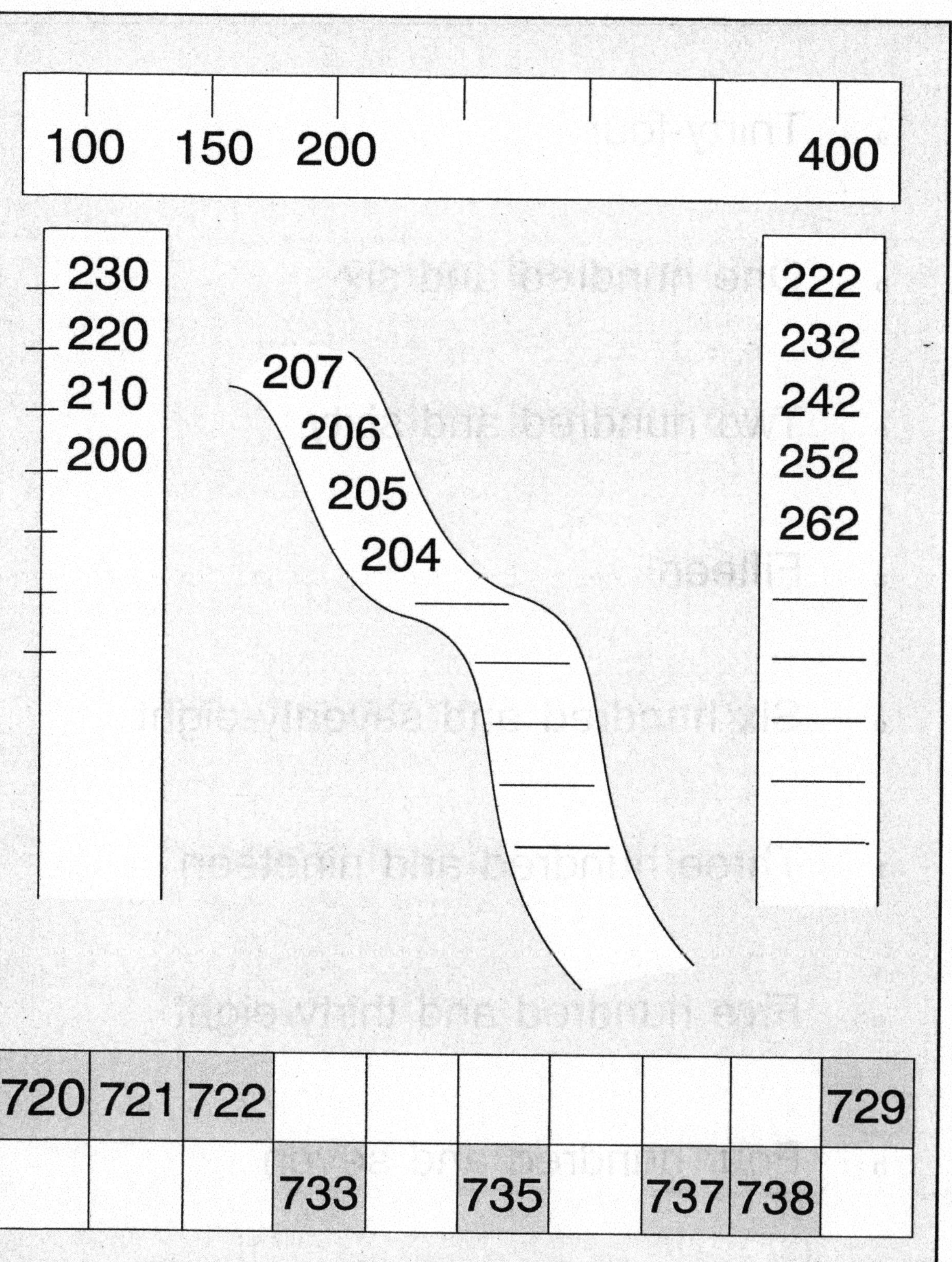
100
150
200
400
230
220
210
200
207
206
205
204
222
232
242
252
262
720
721
722
729
733
735
737
738

a Thirty-four

b One hundred and six

c Two hundred and sixty

d Fifteen

e Six hundred and seventy-eight

f Three hundred and nineteen

g Five hundred and thirty-eight

h Four hundred and seven

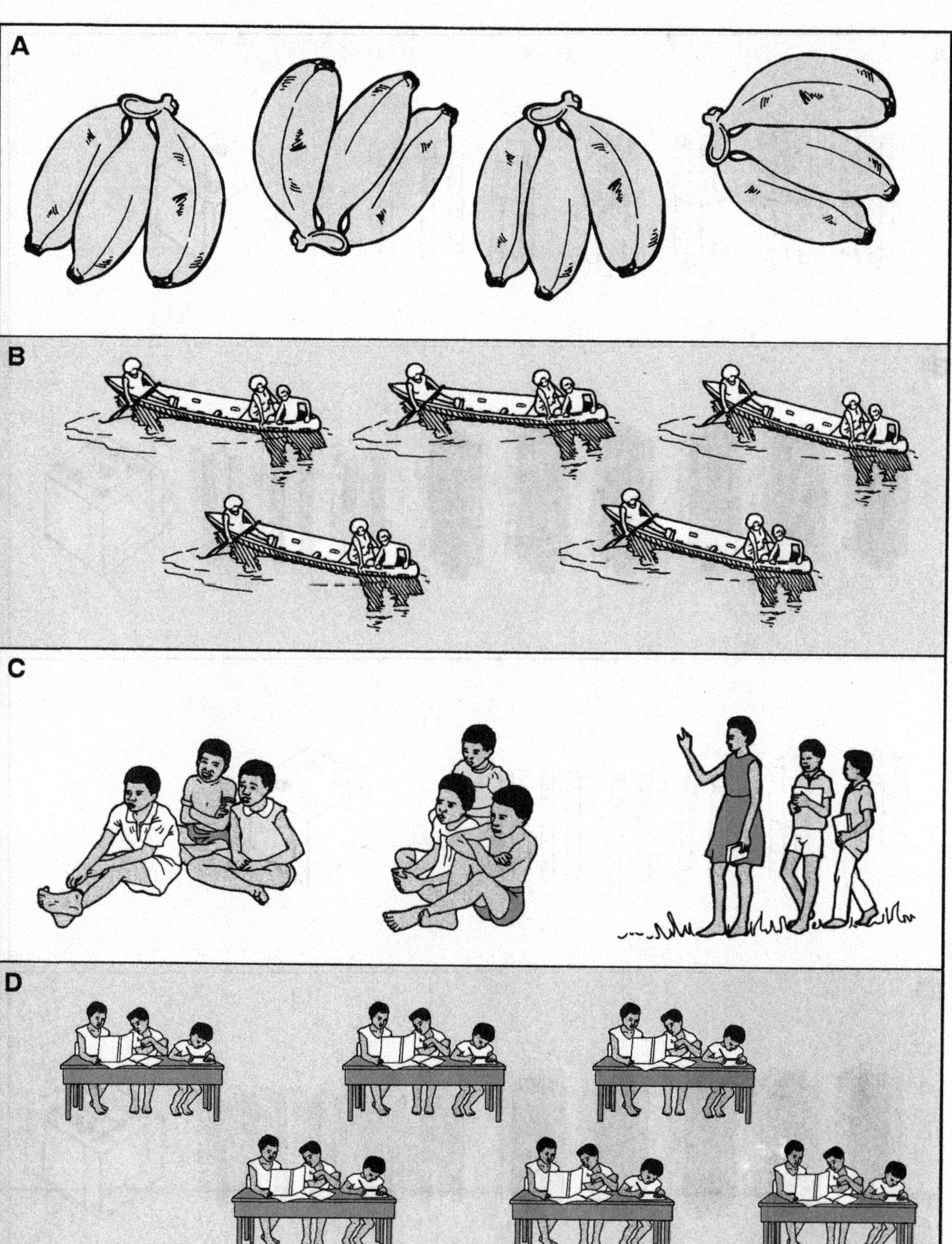
A
B
C
D

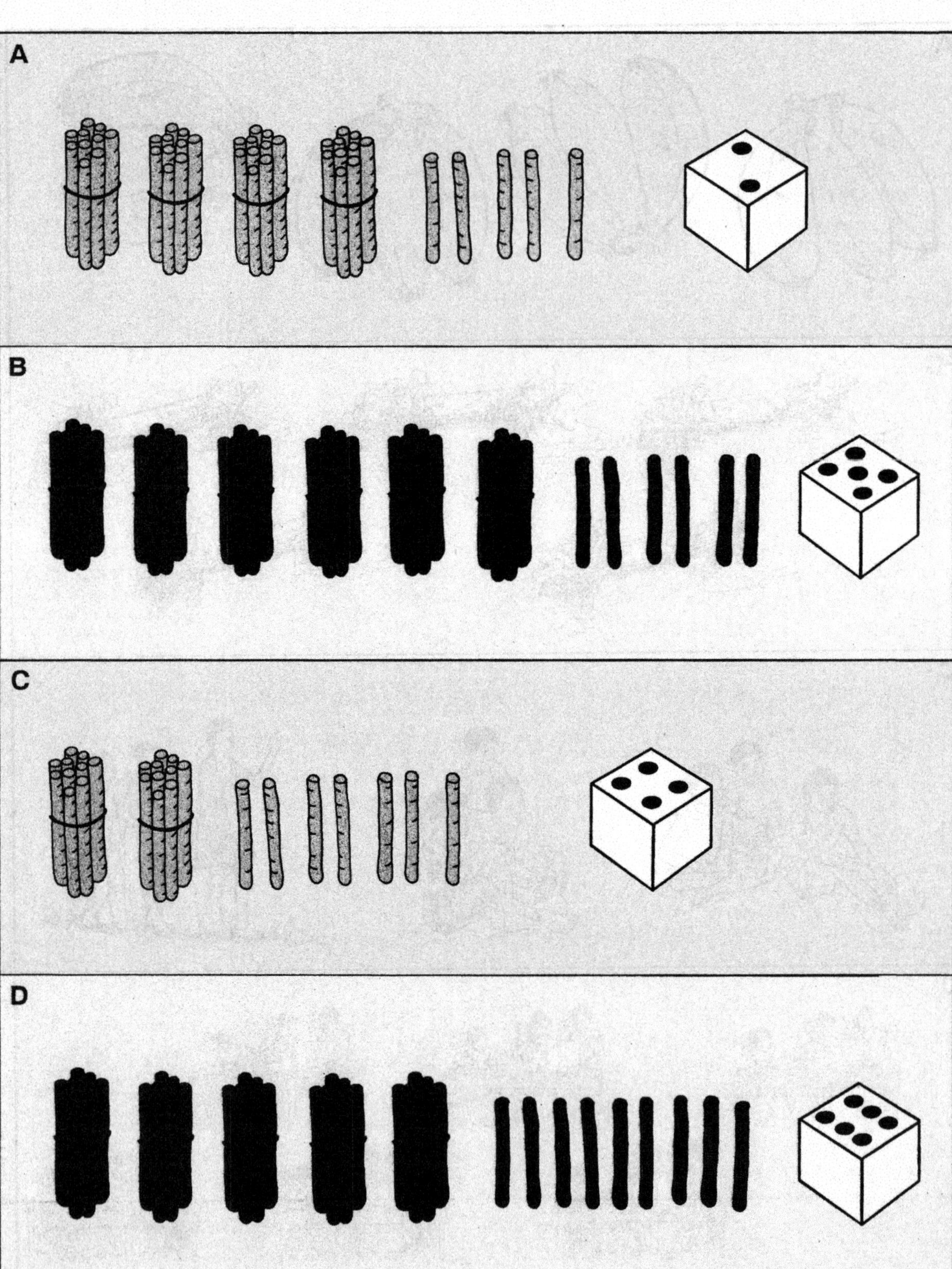
A
B
C
D

a $5 + 3 + 5 =$

b $8 + 4 + 2 =$

c $3 + 7 + 4 =$

d $6 + 4 + 9 =$

e $4 + 7 + 6 =$

f $5 + 5 + 2 =$

g $3 + 4 + 5 =$

h $5 + 6 + 7 =$

i $2 + 2 + 7 =$

j $8 + 8 + 1 + 1 =$

k $6 + 1 + 6 + 1 =$

l $6 + 5 + 6 + 1 =$

m
$$\begin{array}{r} 5 \\ 2 \\ +\ 5 \\ \hline \end{array}$$

n
$$\begin{array}{r} 2 \\ 7 \\ +\ 8 \\ \hline \end{array}$$

o
$$\begin{array}{r} 1 \\ 9 \\ +\ 3 \\ \hline \end{array}$$

p
$$\begin{array}{r} 2 \\ 3 \\ 4 \\ +\ 1 \\ \hline \end{array}$$

q
$$\begin{array}{r} 3 \\ 4 \\ 5 \\ +\ 6 \\ \hline \end{array}$$

r
$$\begin{array}{r} 5 \\ 3 \\ 2 \\ +\ 8 \\ \hline \end{array}$$

a

$$\begin{array}{r} 23 \\ +\ 35 \\ \hline \end{array}$$

b

$$\begin{array}{r} 34 \\ +\ 61 \\ \hline \end{array}$$

c

$$\begin{array}{r} 37 \\ +\ 36 \\ \hline \end{array}$$

d

$$\begin{array}{r} 25 \\ 31 \\ +\ 17 \\ \hline \end{array}$$

e

$$\begin{array}{r} 18 \\ 16 \\ +\ 25 \\ \hline \end{array}$$

f

$$\begin{array}{r} 8 \\ 16 \\ +\ 51 \\ \hline \end{array}$$

g $35 + 67 =$

h $42 + 15 + 91 =$

i $153 + 24 =$

j $171 + 58 =$

k $136 + 27 + 39 =$

a $\begin{array}{r} 134 \\ +\ 456 \\ \hline \end{array}$

b $\begin{array}{r} 286 \\ +\ 147 \\ \hline \end{array}$

c $\begin{array}{r} 158 \\ +\ \ 47 \\ \hline \end{array}$

d $\begin{array}{r} 59 \\ +\ 214 \\ \hline \end{array}$

e $\begin{array}{r} 812 \\ +\ \ 88 \\ \hline \end{array}$

f $\begin{array}{r} 66 \\ +\ 488 \\ \hline \end{array}$

g $\begin{array}{r} 167 \\ 235 \\ +\ \ 21 \\ \hline \end{array}$

h $\begin{array}{r} 115 \\ 87 \\ +\ 421 \\ \hline \end{array}$

i $\begin{array}{r} 67 \\ 251 \\ +\ 377 \\ \hline \end{array}$

j $34 + 29 + 188 =$

k $167 + 341 + 219 =$

TRADE STORE

This weeks specials

PoM - Lae K97
Lae-Goroka K63
Mt Hagan-Madang K68
Lae-Madang K69
PoM-Rabaul K191

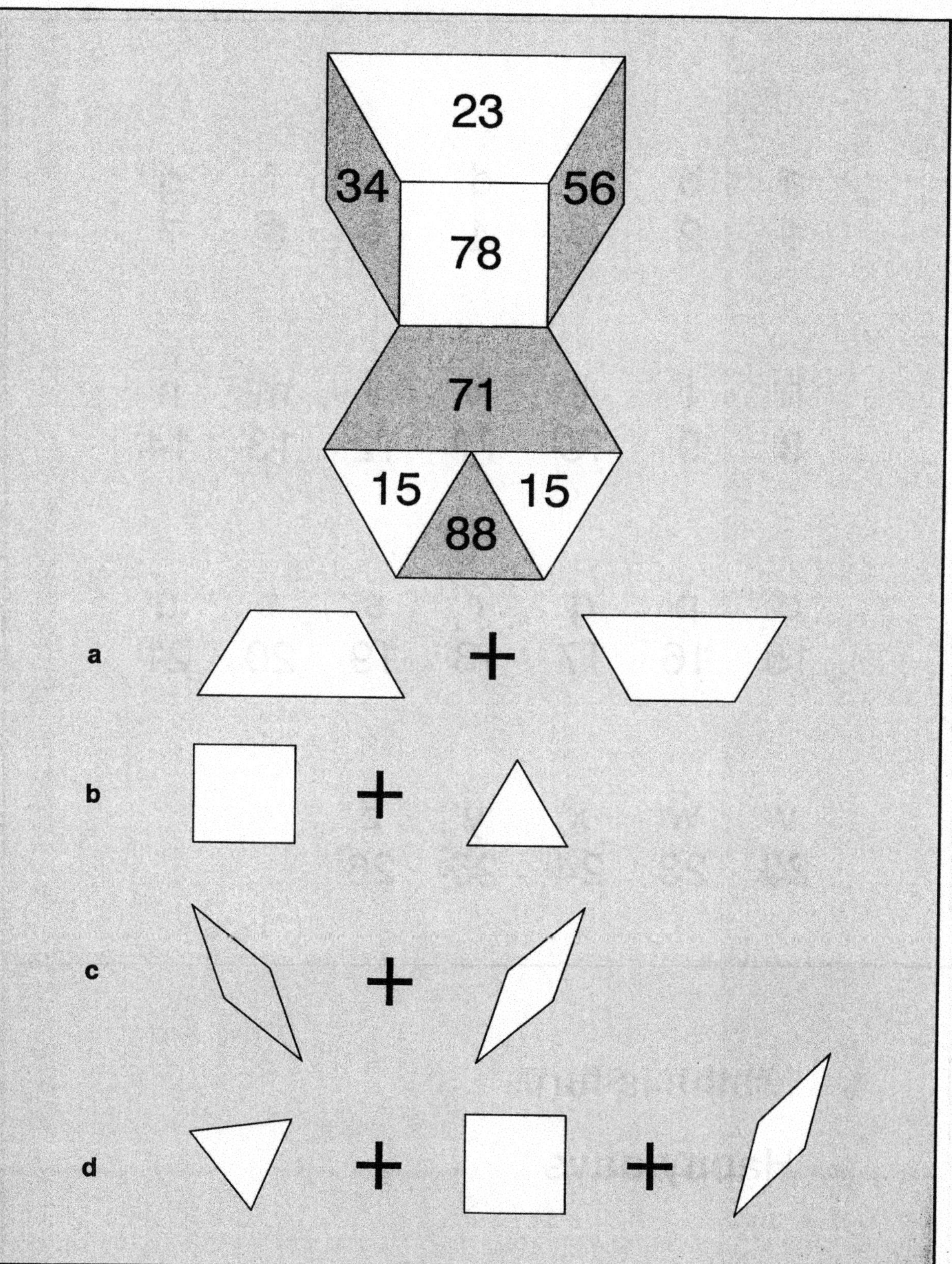
23
34
56
78
71
15
15
88
a
b
c
d

a	b	c	d	e	f	g
1	2	3	4	5	6	7
h	i	j	k	l	m	n
8	9	10	11	12	13	14
o	p	q	r	s	t	u
15	16	17	18	19	20	21
v	w	x	y	z		
22	23	24	25	26		

a Maths is fun.

b Happy days

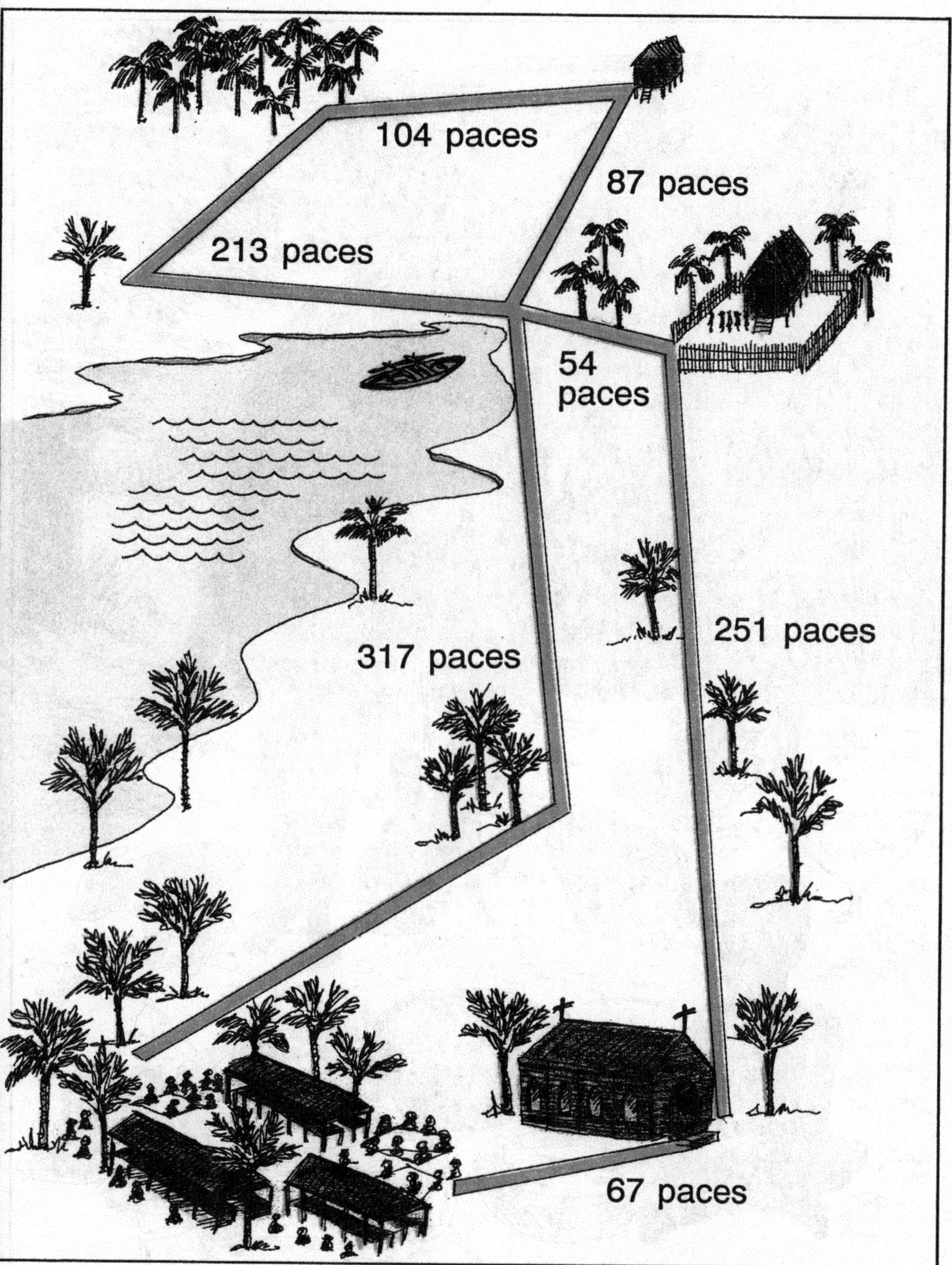
104 paces
87 paces
213 paces
54 paces
251 paces
317 paces
67 paces

HARBOURS

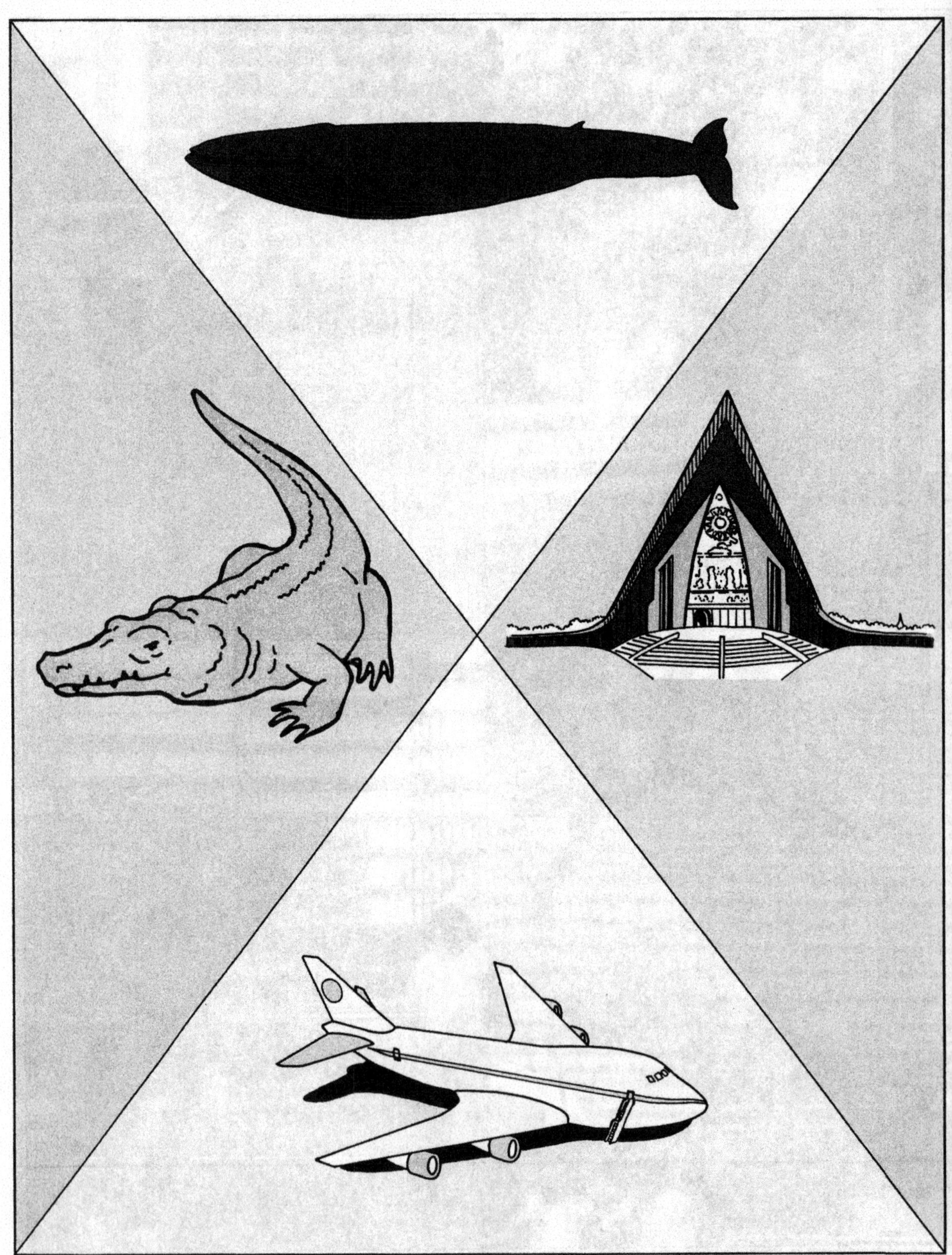

FRESHA
milk
LONGLIFE

A

B

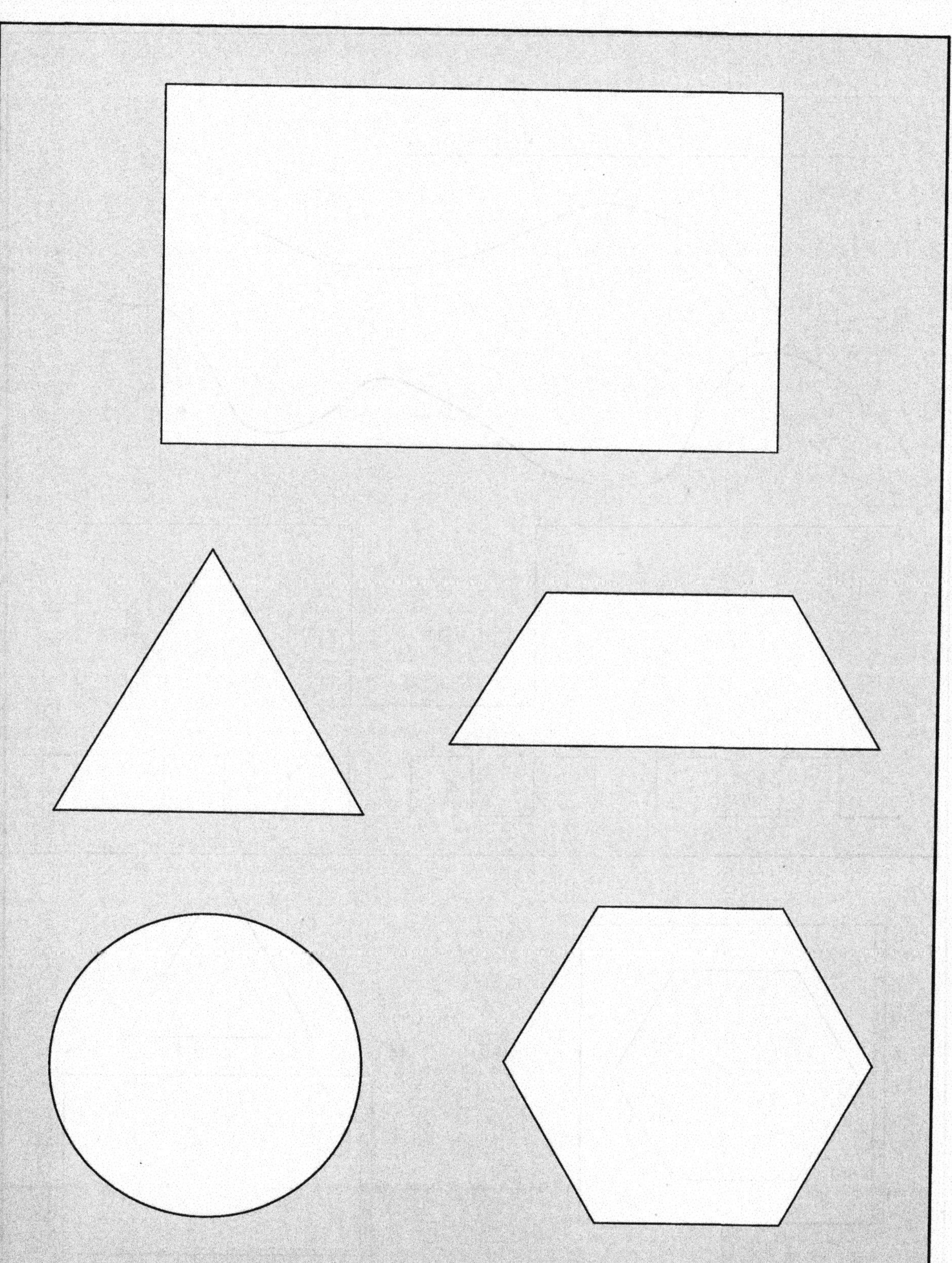

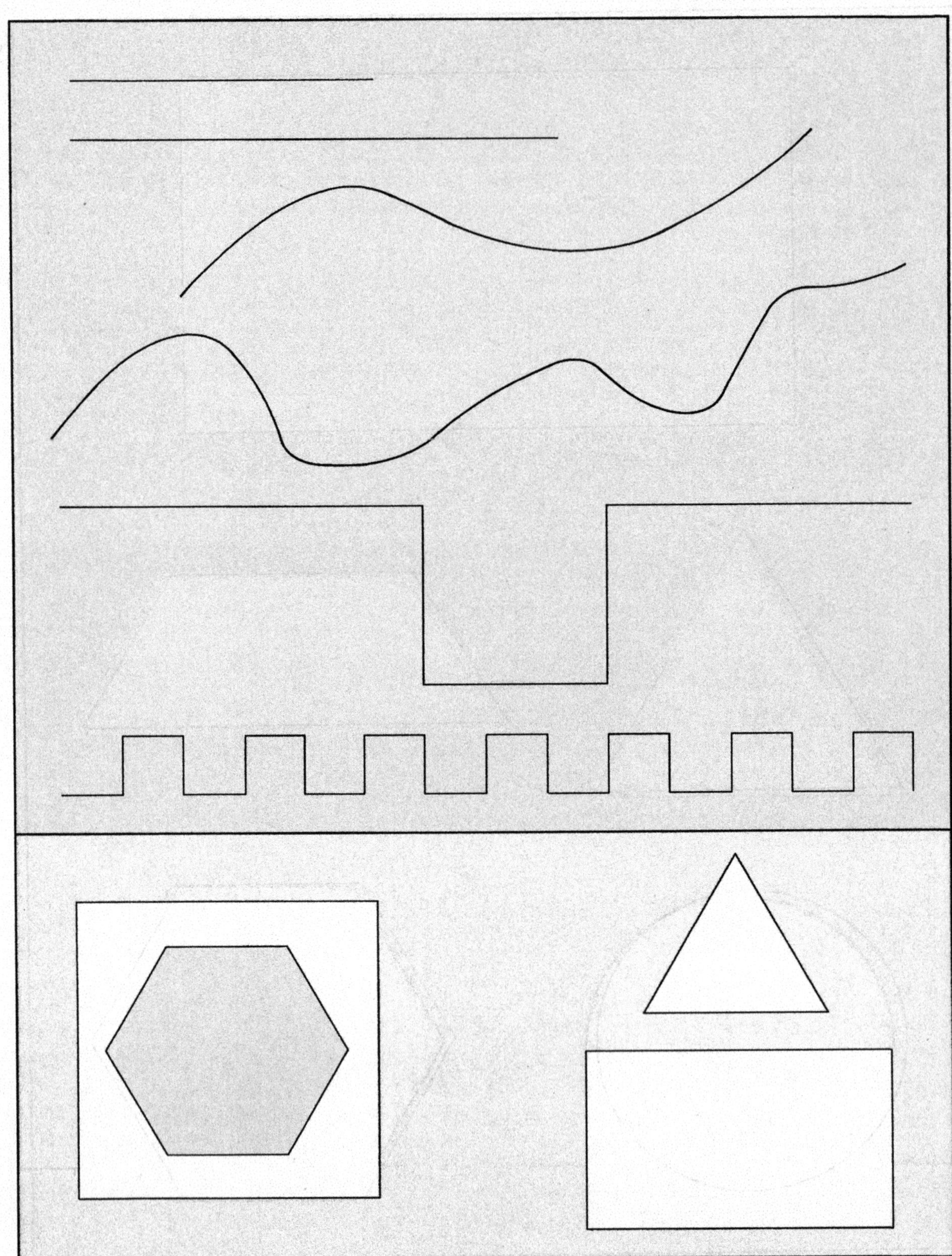

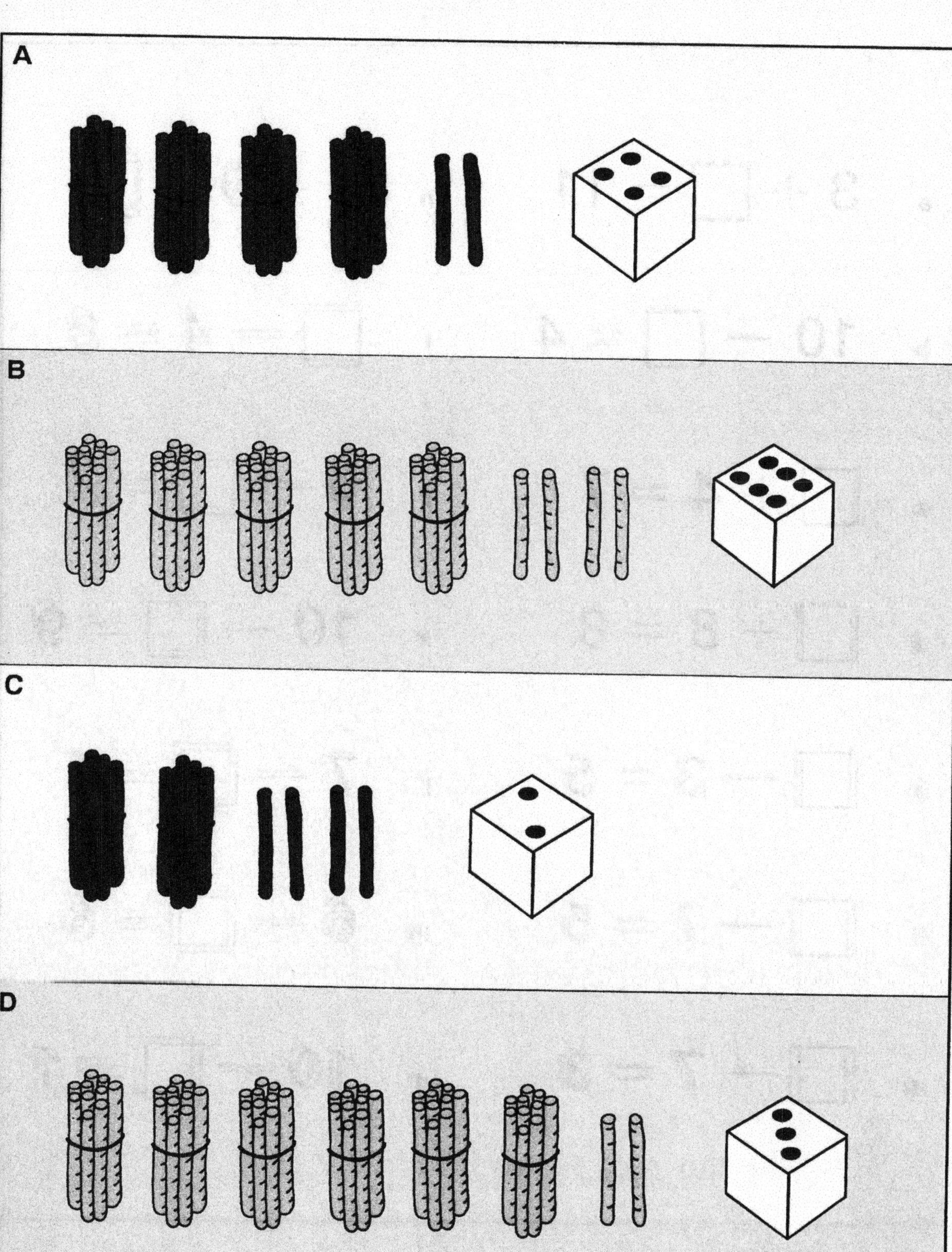
A
B
C
D

a $3 + \square = 11$

b $10 - \square = 4$

c $\square + 4 = 7$

d $\square + 8 = 8$

e $\square - 3 = 5$

f $\square - 7 = 5$

g $\square - 7 = 3$

h $3 + 9 = \square$

i $\square - 4 = 8$

j $6 - \square = 2$

k $10 - \square = 9$

l $7 - \square = 1$

m $6 - \square = 6$

n $10 - \square = 1$

Here are 54 fish

$$54$$

We want to eat 26

$$\begin{array}{r} 54 \\ -\ 26 \\ \hline \end{array}$$

To take away 6
we need to exchange

$$\begin{array}{r} {}^{4}\not{5}{}^{1}4 \\ -\ 26 \\ \hline \end{array}$$

Now we can
take away 6

$$\begin{array}{r} {}^{4}\not{5}{}^{1}4 \\ -\ 26 \\ \hline 8 \end{array}$$

Now we take away 20

$$\begin{array}{r} {}^{4}\not{5}{}^{1}4 \\ -\ 26 \\ \hline 28 \\ \hline \end{array}$$

We have 28 fish left **28**

a $\begin{array}{r} 37 \\ -\ 15 \\ \hline \end{array}$ b $\begin{array}{r} 62 \\ -\ 15 \\ \hline \end{array}$ c $\begin{array}{r} 87 \\ -\ 34 \\ \hline \end{array}$ d $\begin{array}{r} 86 \\ -\ 38 \\ \hline \end{array}$

e $\begin{array}{r} 51 \\ -\ 45 \\ \hline \end{array}$ f $\begin{array}{r} 51 \\ -\ 26 \\ \hline \end{array}$ g $\begin{array}{r} 72 \\ -\ 16 \\ \hline \end{array}$ h $\begin{array}{r} 84 \\ -\ 24 \\ \hline \end{array}$

a $\begin{array}{r} 24 \\ -\ 20 \\ \hline \end{array}$

b $\begin{array}{r} 57 \\ -\ 30 \\ \hline \end{array}$

c $\begin{array}{r} 73 \\ -\ 20 \\ \hline \end{array}$

d $\begin{array}{r} 69 \\ -\ 50 \\ \hline \end{array}$

e $\begin{array}{r} 45 \\ -\ 10 \\ \hline \end{array}$

f $\begin{array}{r} 91 \\ -\ 40 \\ \hline \end{array}$

g $\begin{array}{r} 20 \\ -\ 16 \\ \hline \end{array}$

h $\begin{array}{r} 50 \\ -\ 24 \\ \hline \end{array}$

i $\begin{array}{r} 60 \\ -\ 17 \\ \hline \end{array}$

j $\begin{array}{r} 80 \\ -\ 52 \\ \hline \end{array}$

k $\begin{array}{r} 80 \\ -\ 58 \\ \hline \end{array}$

l $\begin{array}{r} 90 \\ -\ 67 \\ \hline \end{array}$

a
$$\begin{array}{r} 456 \\ -\ 127 \\ \hline \end{array}$$

b
$$\begin{array}{r} 129 \\ -\ 54 \\ \hline \end{array}$$

c
$$\begin{array}{r} 328 \\ -\ 182 \\ \hline \end{array}$$

d
$$\begin{array}{r} 671 \\ -\ 80 \\ \hline \end{array}$$

e
$$\begin{array}{r} 452 \\ -\ 187 \\ \hline \end{array}$$

f
$$\begin{array}{r} 391 \\ -\ 269 \\ \hline \end{array}$$

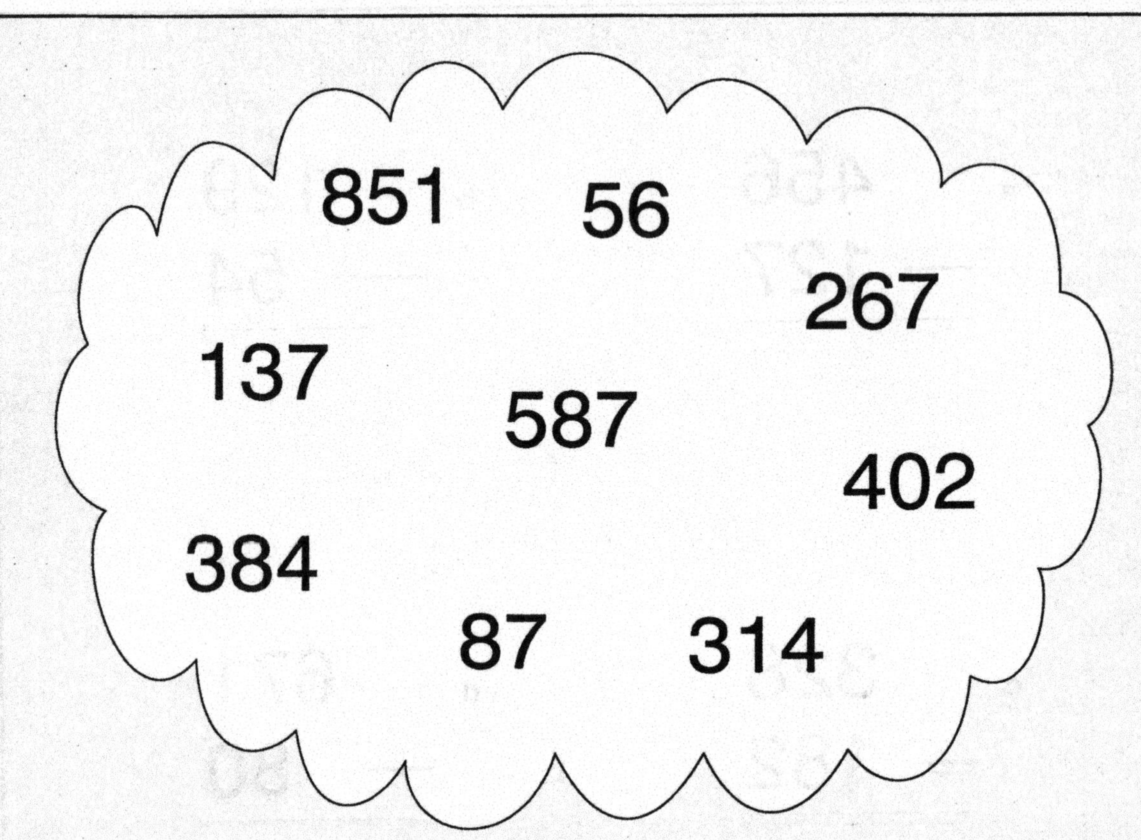

50	227	449	18
117	795	531	273
328	500	450	88
135	81	297	203

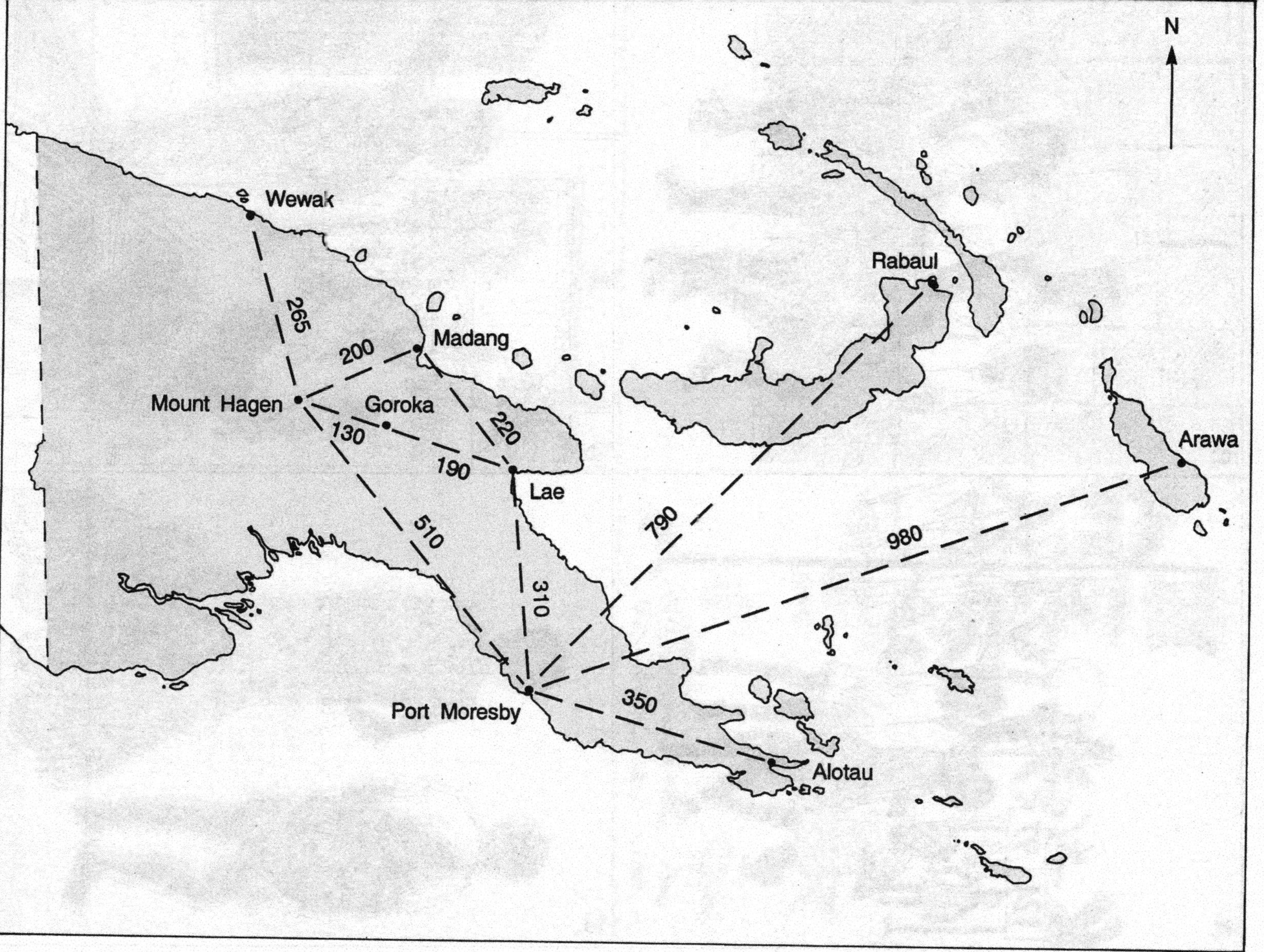
N
Wewak
Rabaul
265
200
Madang
Mount Hagen
Goroka
220
130
190
Arawa
Lae
790
510
980
310
350
Port Moresby
Alotau

A
124
97
B
C
D

A

$$\begin{array}{r} 3\square \\ -\ 27 \\ \hline 8 \end{array}$$

B

$$\begin{array}{r} 2\square 4 \\ -\ 12\square \\ \hline 88 \end{array}$$

C

$\square - \square = 1$

$\square - \square = 2$

$\square - \square = 10$

$\square - \square = 75$

A
B
C
D
E
F

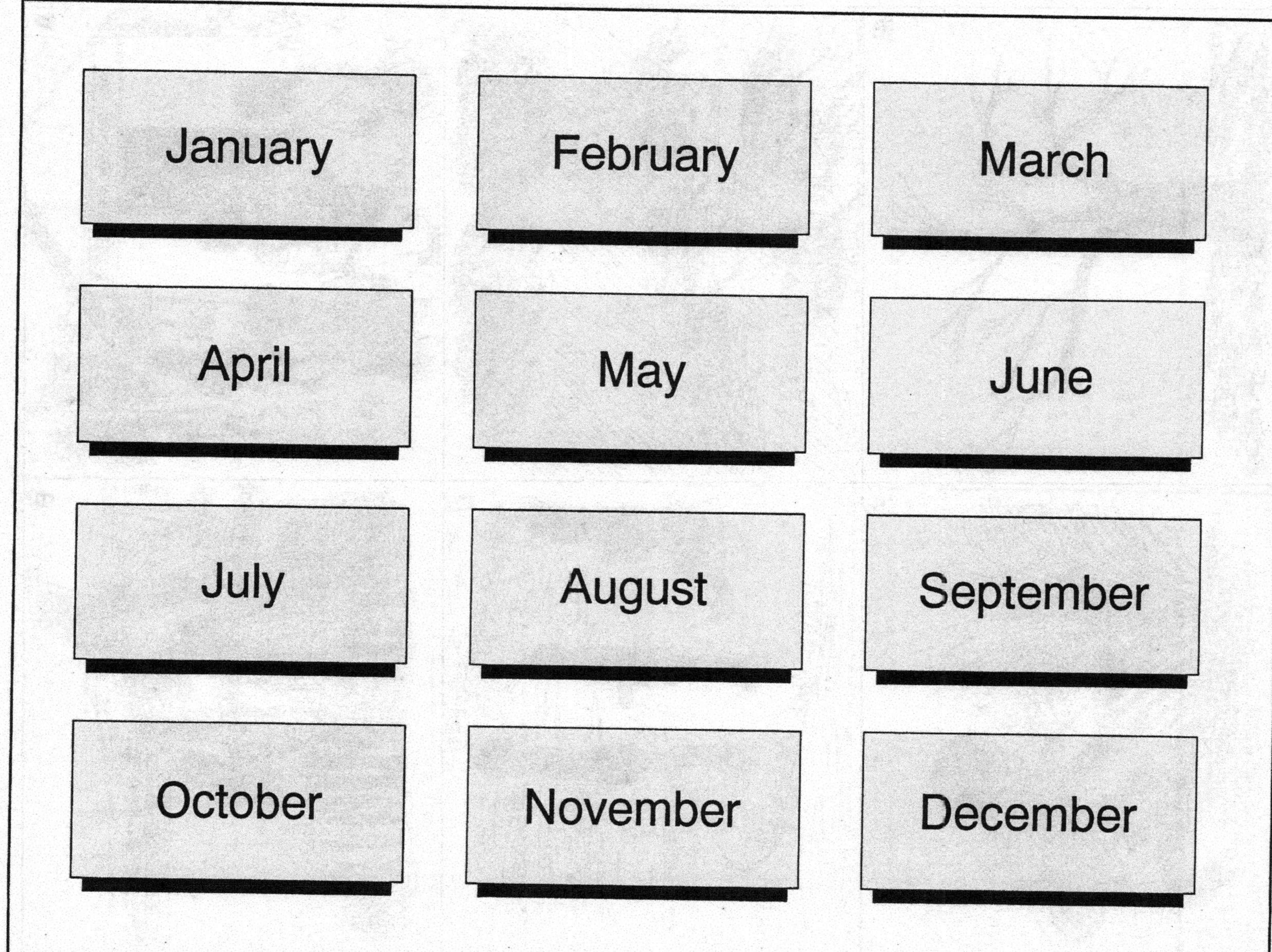
January
February
March
April
May
June
July
August
September
October
November
December

A
PAY SCHOOL FEES HERE
B
TALAIR
C
D
E
F

Year 2000

January

S	M	T	W	T	F	S
30	31					1
2	3	4	5	6	7	8
9	10	11	12	13	14	15
16	17	18	19	20	21	22
23	24	25	26	27	28	29

February

S	M	T	W	T	F	S
		1	2	3	4	5
6	7	8	9	10	11	12
13	14	15	16	17	18	19
20	21	22	23	24	25	26
27	28	29				

March

S	M	T	W	T	F	S
			1	2	3	4
5	6	7	8	9	10	11
12	13	14	15	16	17	18
19	20	21	22	23	24	25
26	27	28	29	30	31	

April

S	M	T	W	T	F	S
30						1
2	3	4	5	6	7	8
9	10	11	12	13	14	15
16	17	18	19	20	21	22
23	24	25	26	27	28	29

May

S	M	T	W	T	F	S
	1	2	3	4	5	6
7	8	9	10	11	12	13
14	15	16	17	18	19	20
21	22	23	24	25	26	27
28	29	30	31			

June

S	M	T	W	T	F	S
				1	2	3
4	5	6	7	8	9	10
11	12	13	14	15	16	17
18	19	20	21	22	23	24
25	26	27	28	29	30	

July

S	M	T	W	T	F	S
30	31					1
2	3	4	5	6	7	8
9	10	11	12	13	14	15
16	17	18	19	20	21	22
23	24	25	26	27	28	29

August

S	M	T	W	T	F	S
		1	2	3	4	5
6	7	8	9	10	11	12
13	14	15	16	17	18	19
20	21	22	23	24	25	26
27	28	29	30	31		

September

S	M	T	W	T	F	S
					1	2
3	4	5	6	7	8	9
10	11	12	13	14	15	16
17	18	19	20	21	22	23
24	25	26	27	28	29	30

October

S	M	T	W	T	F	S
1	2	3	4	5	6	7
8	9	10	11	12	13	14
15	16	17	18	19	20	21
22	23	24	25	26	27	28
29	30	31				

November

S	M	T	W	T	F	S
			1	2	3	4
5	6	7	8	9	10	11
12	13	14	15	16	17	18
19	20	21	22	23	24	25
26	27	28	29	30		

December

S	M	T	W	T	F	S
31					1	2
3	4	5	6	7	8	9
10	11	12	13	14	15	16
17	18	19	20	21	22	23
24	25	26	27	28	29	30

Sunday	Monday	Tuesday	Wednesday	Thursday	Friday	Saturday
1	2	3	4	5	6	7
8	9	10	11	12	13	14
15	16	17	18	19	20	21
22	23	24	25	26	27	28
29	30					

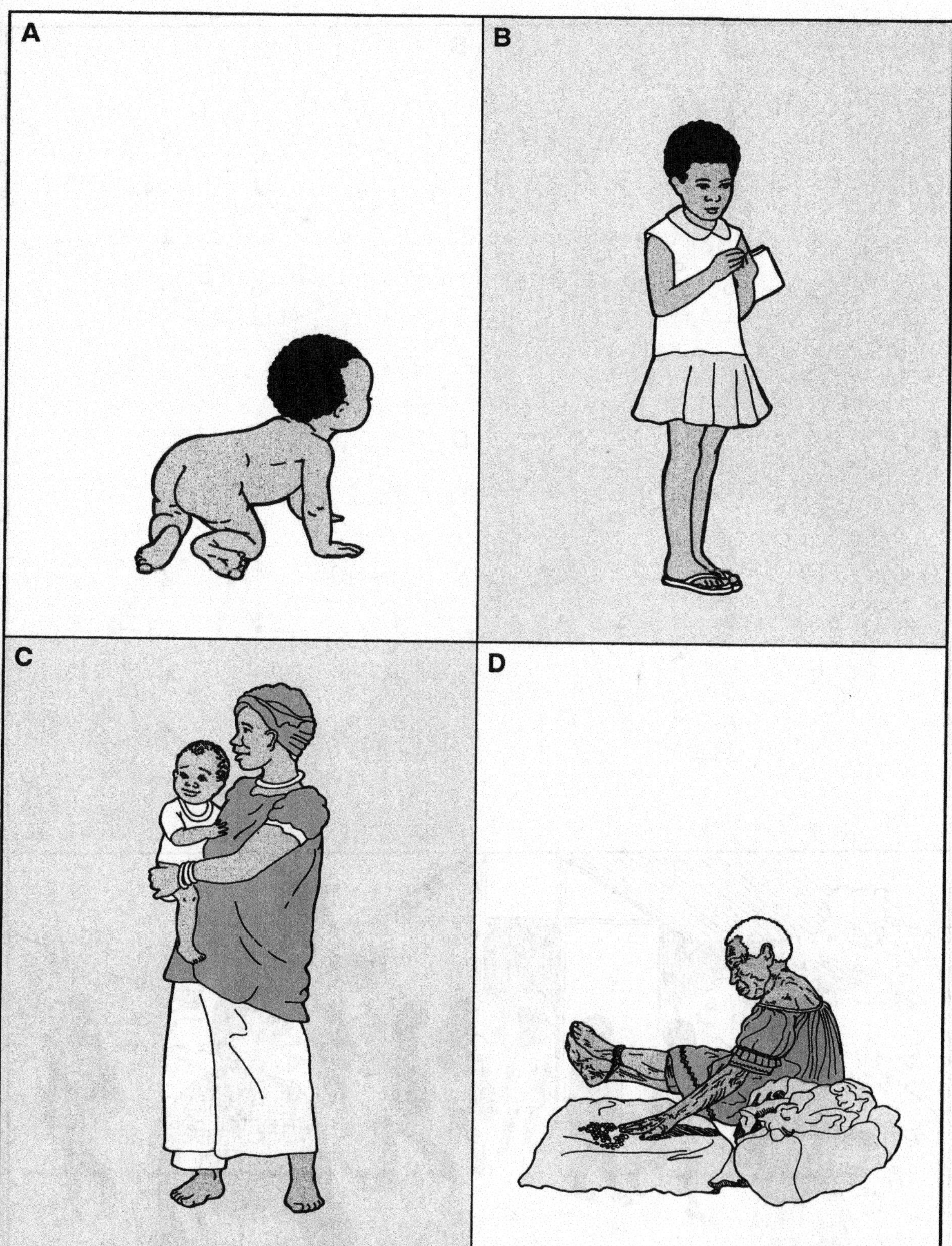
A
B
C
D

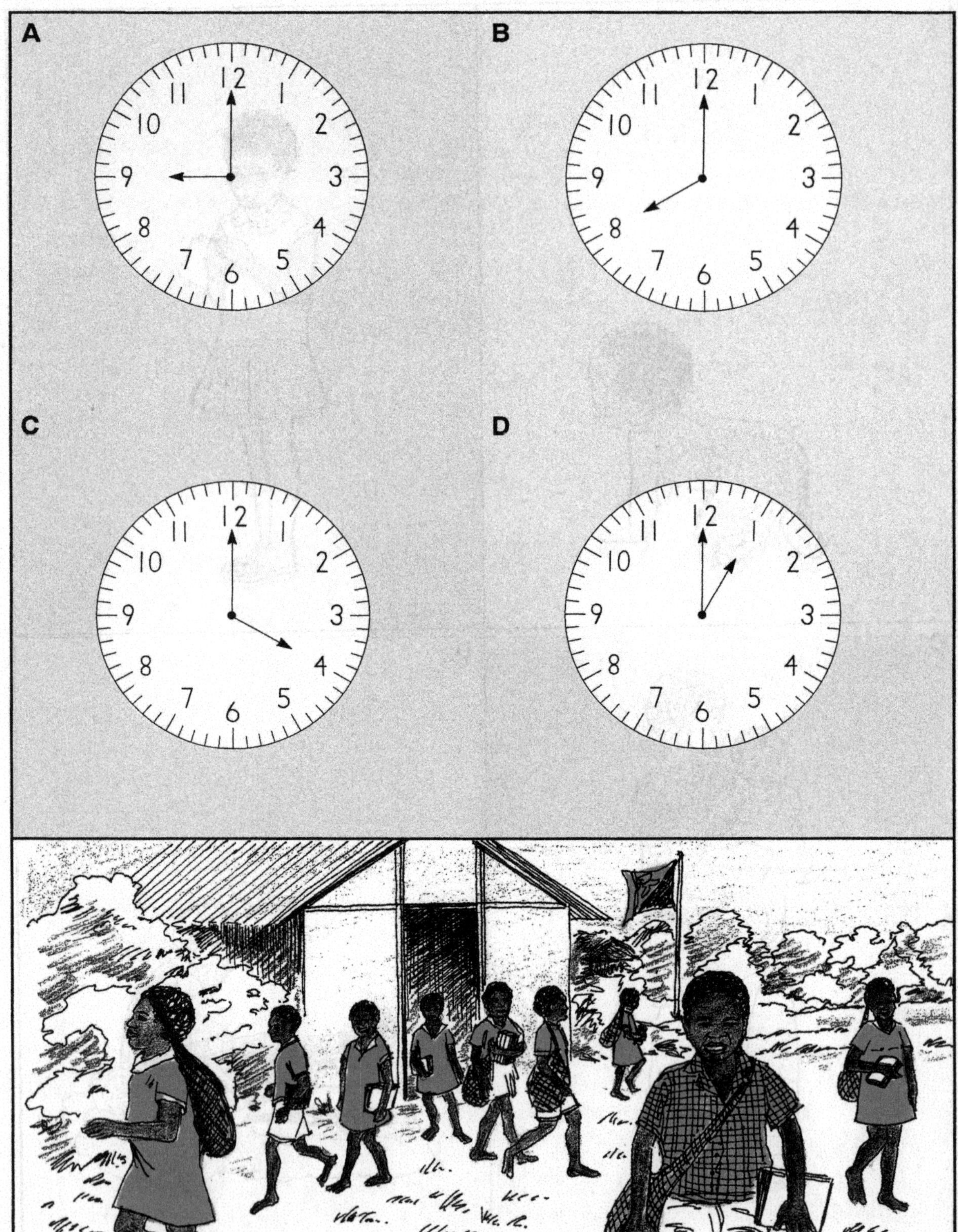
A
B
C
D

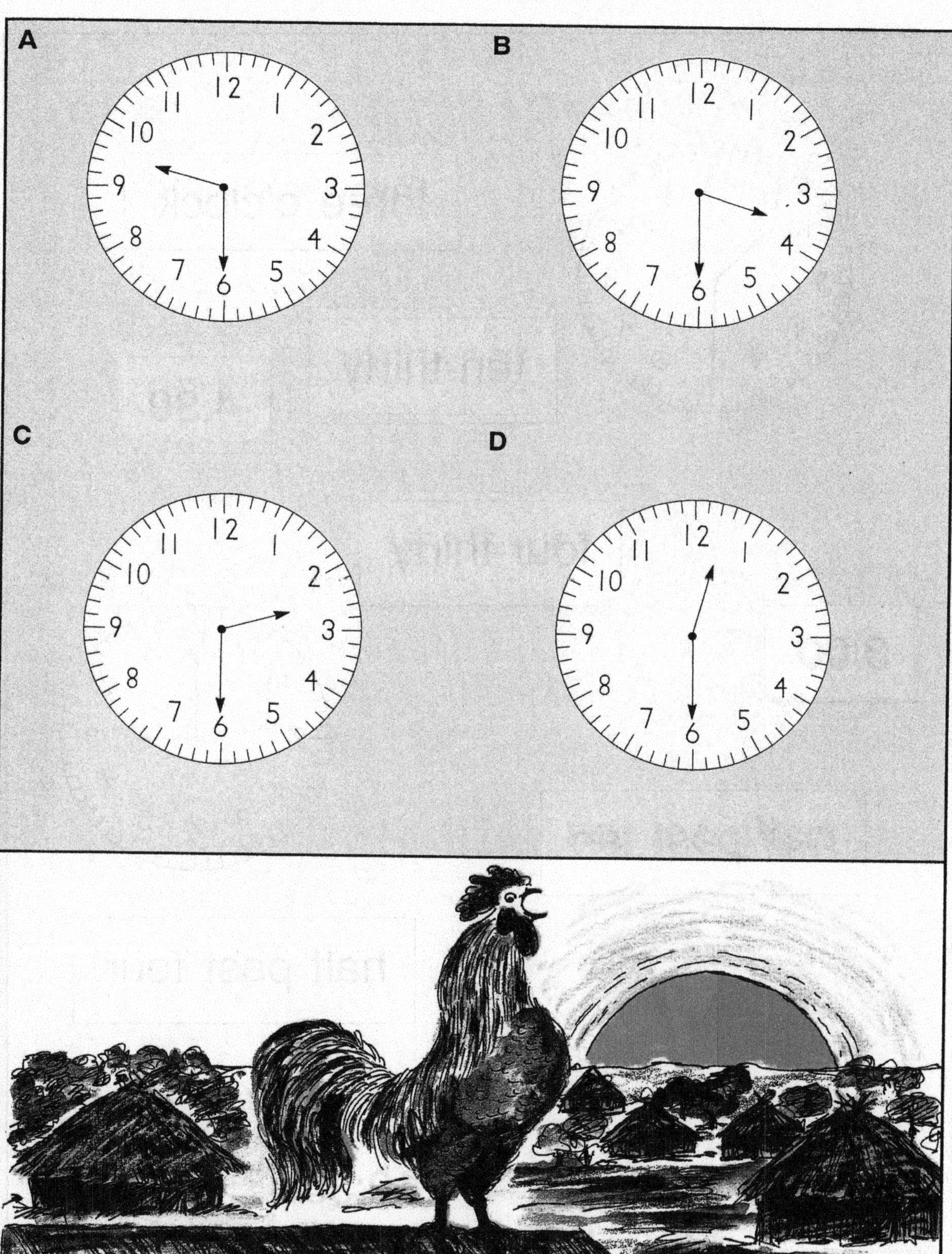
A
B
C
D

three o'clock
ten-thirty
4:30
four-thirty
3:00
half past ten
half past four
10:30

6:30
5:00
AM
FM
10:30

A
B
C

A
B
C
D

A
B
C
D
E
F

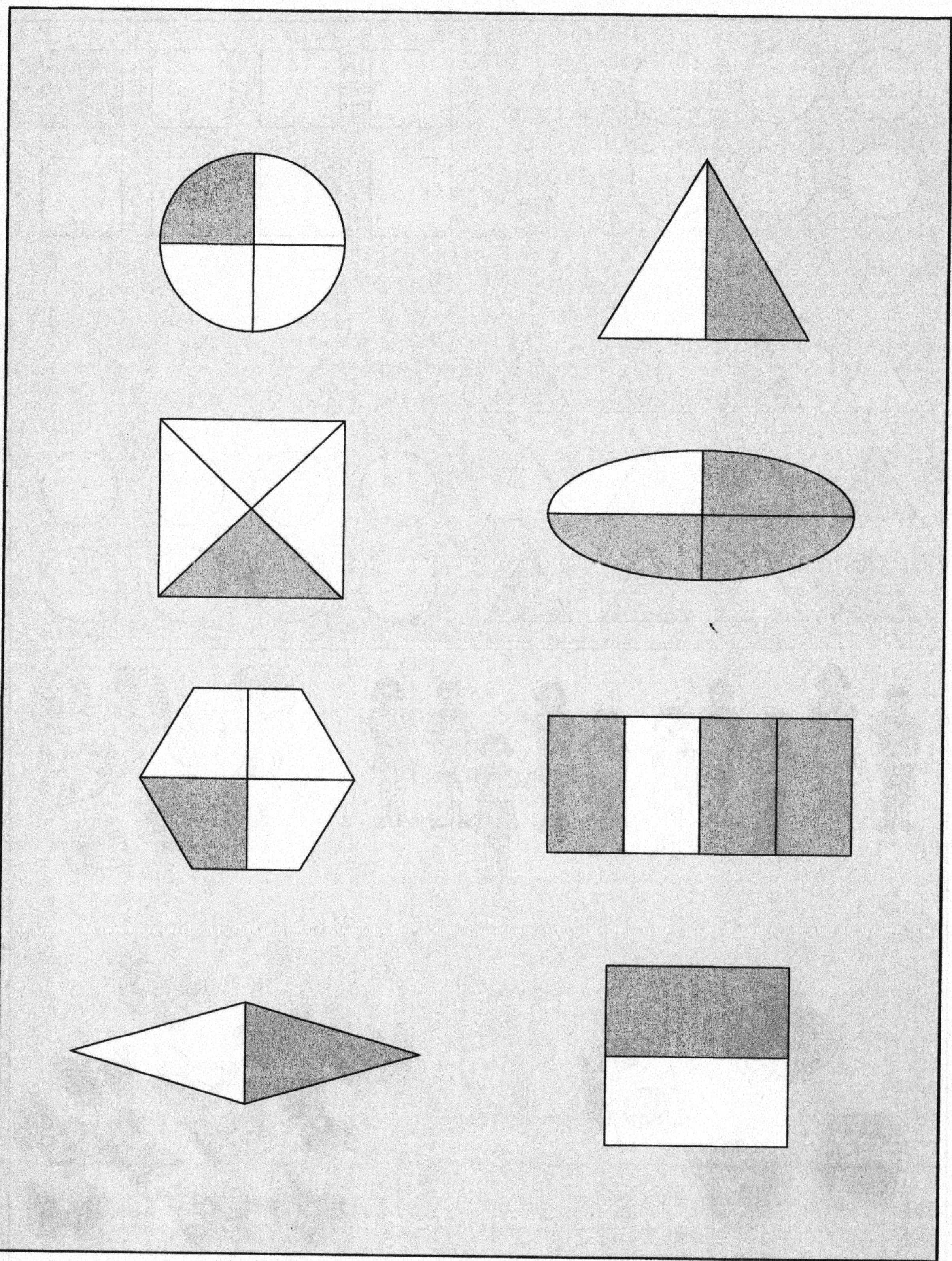

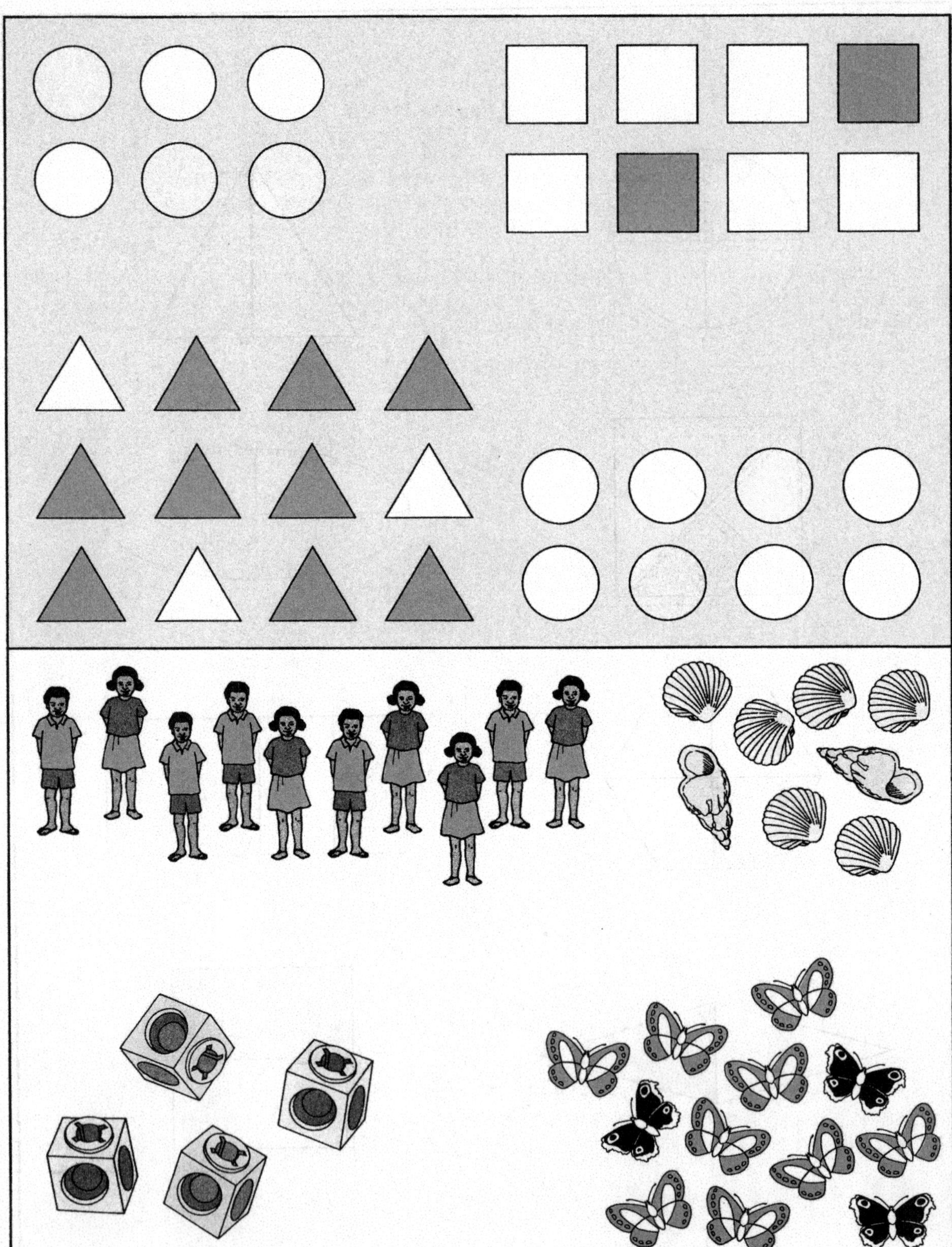

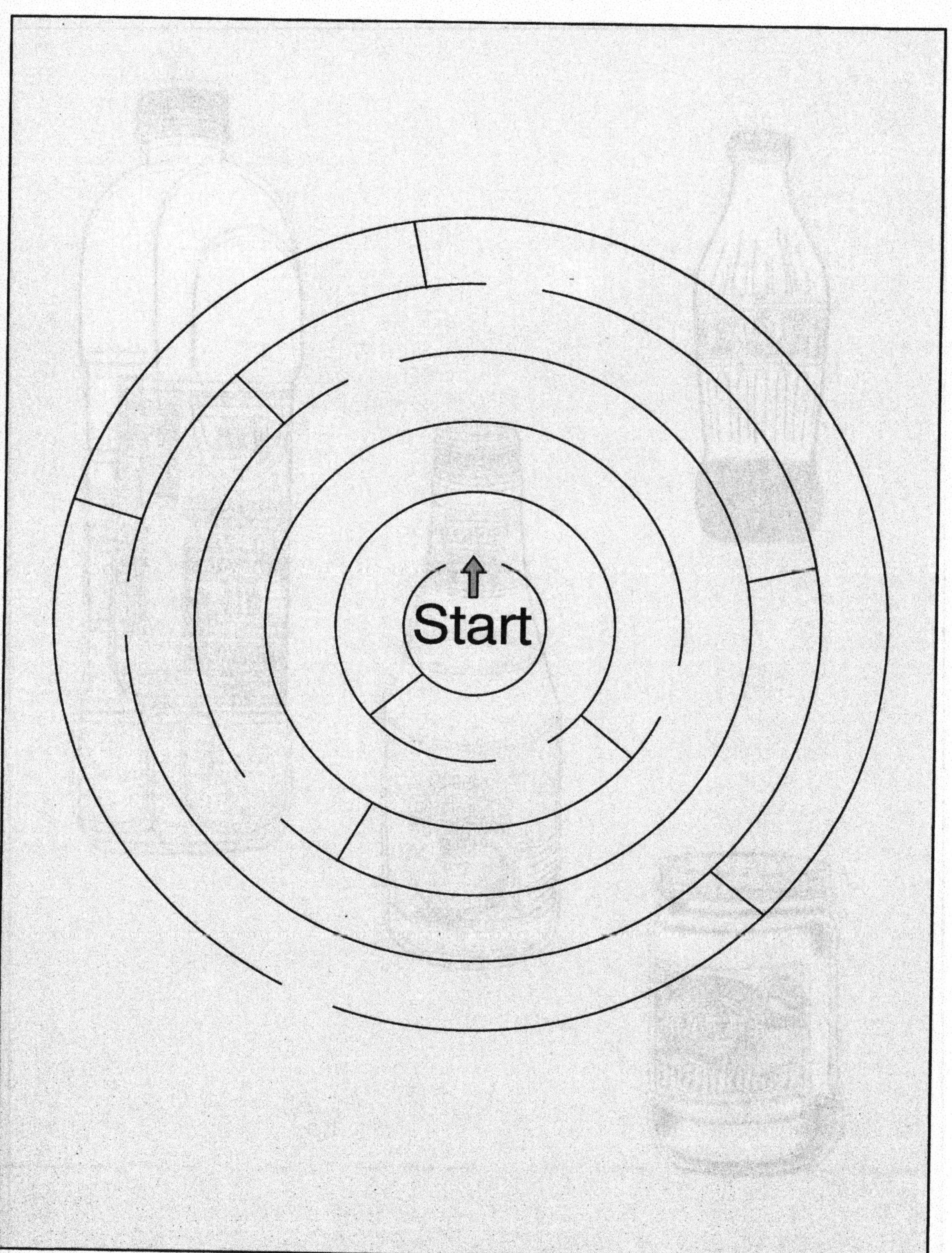
Start

300ml
Coke

HEINZ
HEINZ
BIG RED
TOMATO SAUCE
600ml

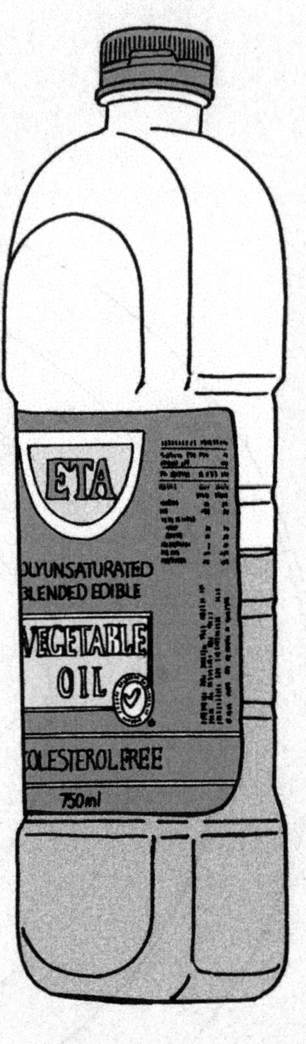
ETA
OLYUNSATURATED
BLENDED EDIBLE
VEGETABLE
OIL
COLESTEROL FREE
750ml

CRUNCHY
E·T·A
Peanut Butte

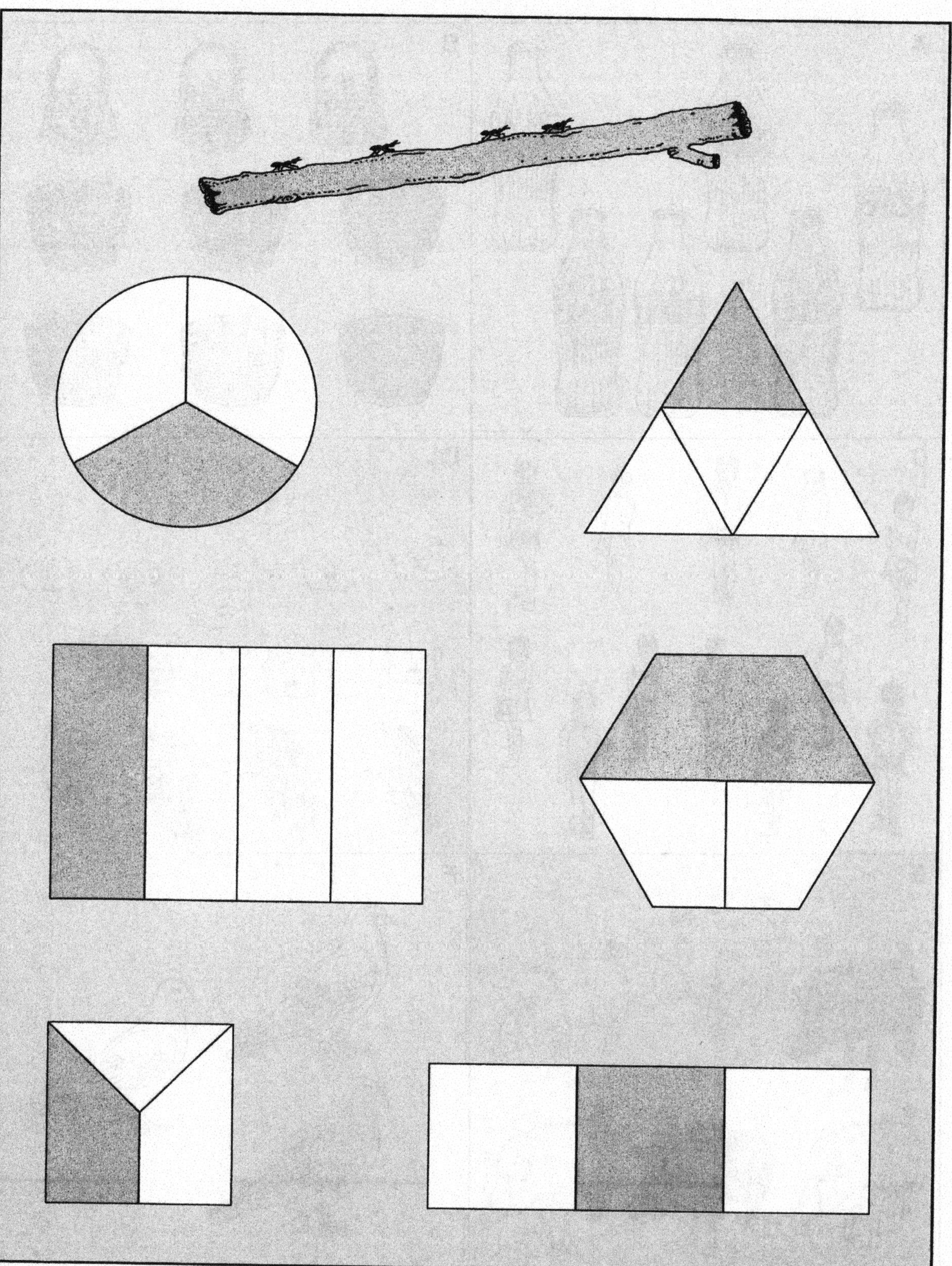

A
B
C
D
E
F

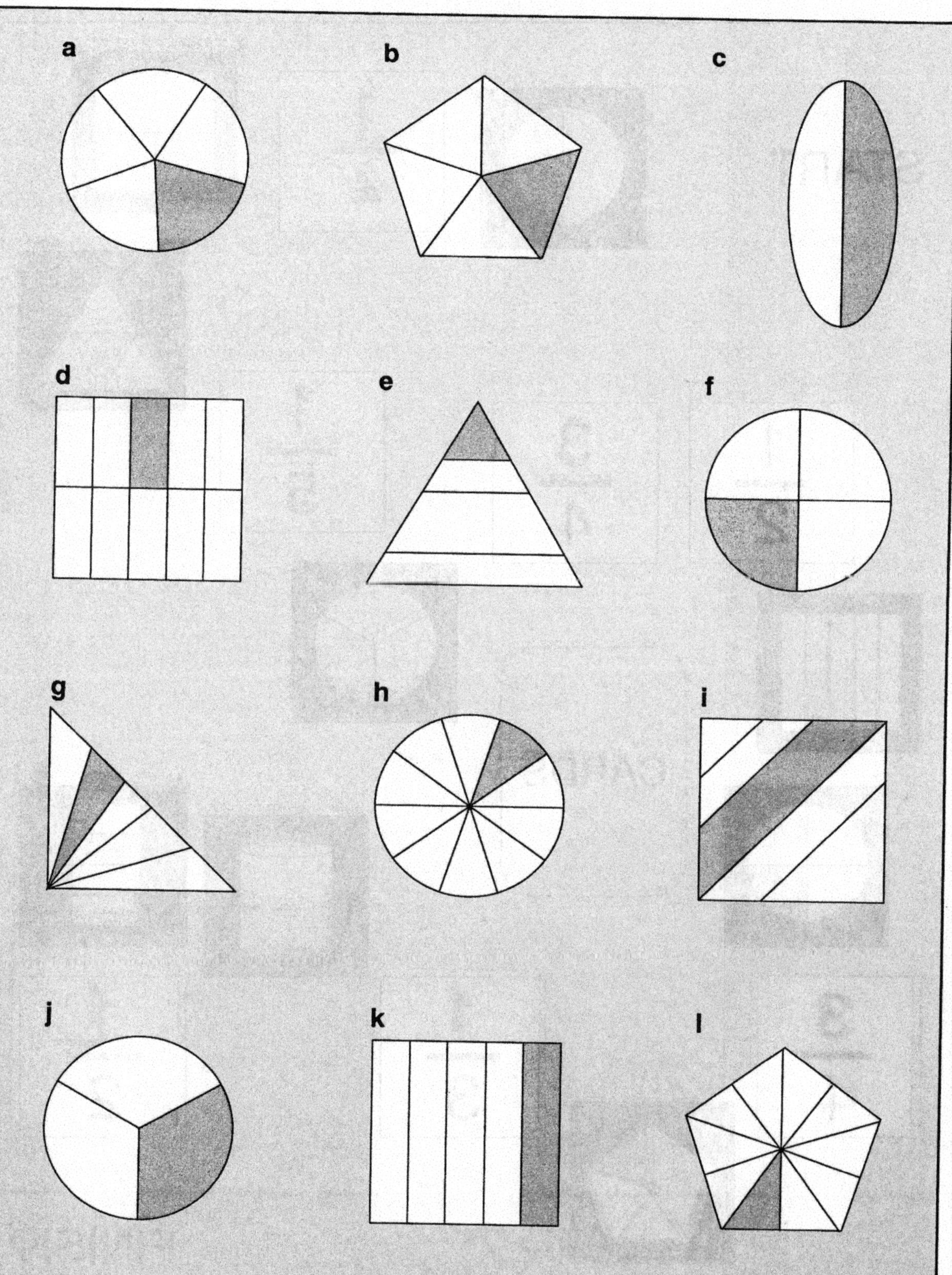
a
b
c
d
e
f
g
h
i
j
k
l

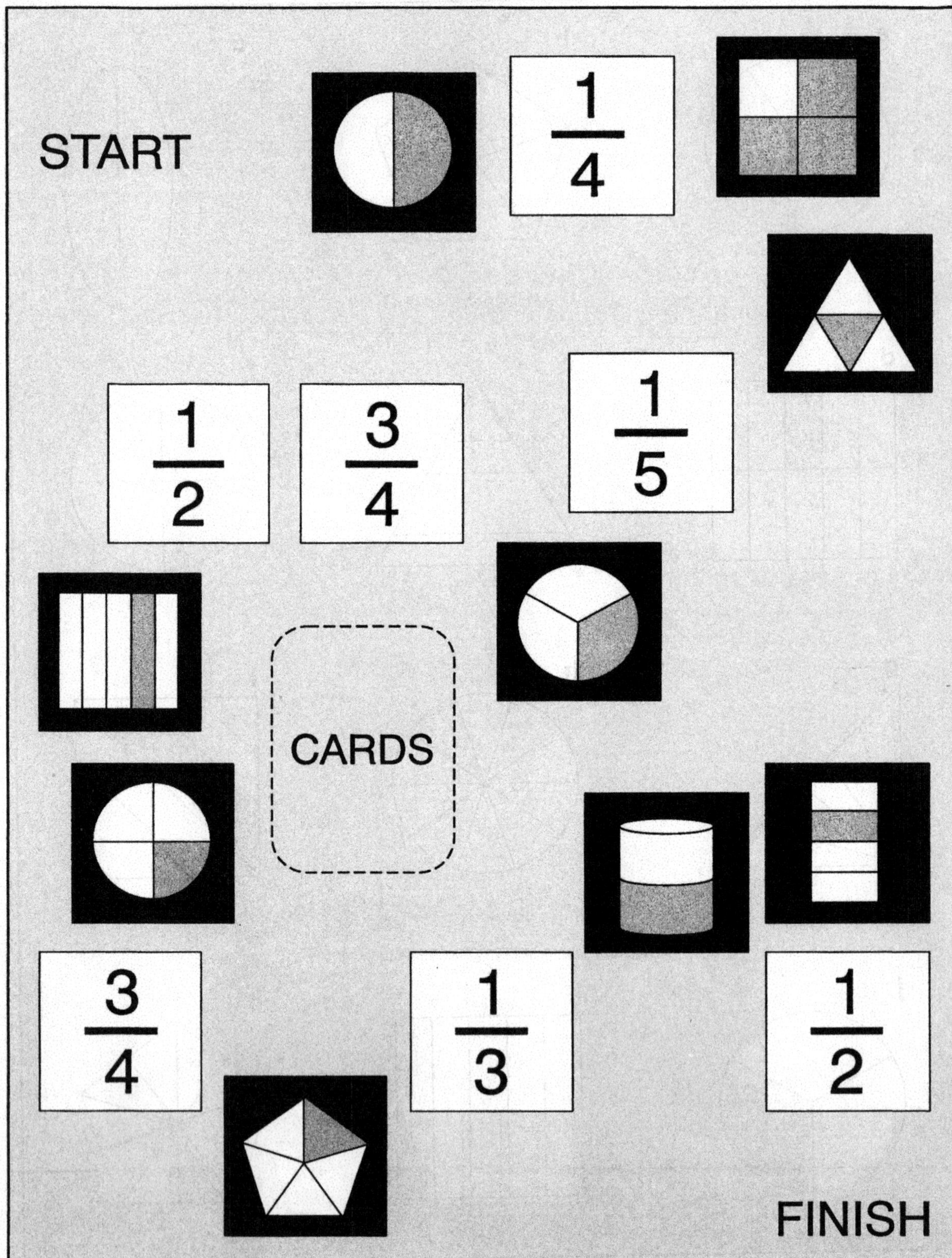
START
1/4
3/4
1/2
1/5
CARDS
3/4
1/3
1/2
FINISH